Essays on Poetry

A

Essays on Poetry

By J. C. Squire

John Collings

Essay Index Reprint Series

BOOKS FOR LIBRARIES PRESS, INC.

FREEPORT, NEW YORK

First Published 1923
Reprinted 1967

PN
1136
S7
1967

LIBRARY OF CONGRESS CATALOG CARD NUMBER:
67-26787

PRINTED IN THE UNITED STATES OF AMERICA

TO
OSWALD P. MILNE

PREFATORY NOTE

THE first two papers in this volume were delivered as lectures at the Royal Institution on February 3rd and 10th, 1923. They were spoken from brief notes ; the shorthand report has been, in places, emended ; but the lectures have been left as lectures. I found that if I attempted to alter them I should expand them indefinitely. Of the others, the majority appeared in *The London Mercury*, and most of the rest in *The Observer*, to whose editor I am grateful. One was a preface to Mr. I. A. Williams' *Byways round Helicon*, which Messrs. Heinemann allow me to reprint. The paper on Tennyson was printed two years before the publication of two books which have recently recalled attention to his work. The connection of the last essay, which is nominally about prose, with the others will be evident to anybody who is at the pains to read it.

J. C. S.

CONTENTS

SUBJECT IN POETRY

I

THE question before us this afternoon,* as it will be the question next Saturday, is " Subject in Poetry, with a special relation to Contemporary Poetry." With your permission, ladies and gentlemen, I shall confine myself chiefly this afternoon to the first half of that topic and deal specially with emotional influence. I shall speak of change in subject, and the introduction of new subjects next week, though I cannot be certain that anybody who is here to-day will be here next week.

I suppose it is impossible—at any rate, I feel it to be impossible in surroundings with the scientific traditions of these—to enter upon a disquisition on any subject without, I won't say some attempt at definition, but, at any rate, some recognition that definitions exist, some reference to definition : and I feel that I simply must begin, although I shall not go very far with that matter, by asking " What is Poetry ? " and " What is Subject ? "

" What is Poetry ? " Ladies and gentlemen, a great many definitions have been attempted, and I think that they have only had this one thing in common : that none of them is comprehensive, and that those who have attempted them have uniformly quarrelled with each other's attempts. Man after man has endeavoured to make a definition of Poetry.

* These two papers were delivered as lectures at the Royal Institution, on February 10th and 17th, 1923. See Prefatory Note.

It was attempted by Wordsworth : it was attempted by Coleridge (who very likely tried it within these walls, which he entered on several occasions), and it was attempted by Matthew Arnold : contributions to the subject have been made by Gabriel Rossetti, and a great many others, but one man has dealt specifically with one aspect of the question and one with another. One has insisted on the emotional aspect of Poetry, one on the artistic : one on the content, one on the method of expression ; but, up to the present date, no adequate definition of poetry, no complete, no inclusive and exclusive definition has been made, and, for myself, I do not mind confessing that I doubt if any man ever will make one. The consequence is that, when we talk about poetry, we are not in a position to talk about a thing the precise nature of which we can look up in a work of reference. We talk merely about a class of works which, by general assent of mankind, have been given a particular name.

We live in an age which is inclined to ask questions. It has been said by Mr. Chesterton, a very wise if sometimes rather a flippant man, that this age is very interested in asking questions, but not in listening to the answers, particularly if these are old answers. If this is a proclivity which has been observable in the political, social and moral spheres, we have also seen it operating very extensively in the sphere of æsthetics, and in that of literature. Persons have produced works over which there has been a great deal of controversy, works to which most of us have felt inclined to deny the title of poetry, and when they have been told that we were unwilling to accept these works as poetry, their answer has been : " We call this poetry, and if we choose to call this poetry, who can prevent us ? " Well, if that were a position that could be accepted, it would be good-bye to definitions, and it would be an end of discussion. We have to take it, I think, that just as we allow any other word which cannot be precisely defined, like " giraffe " or " elephant," to be applied to an object which we recognise when we see it as belonging to that class of objects, which has been given that name by mankind throughout the ages, we have to agree that the particular word poetry should go on being applied to that class of objects which has always been accorded the name, and that if anybody produces something different, however worthy, another word should be invented for it. Therefore, when I consider poetry, when I consider, as I am this afternoon considering, " Subject in Poetry," I am content to say that poetry, whatever it is or is not, is a certain body of works which we have inherited from the past, and to which mankind in all ages has agreed in giving this name, and any other works, present or future, which bear all the obvious marks present in that body of writing. I can only say that Homer's poetry, and Sophocles' poetry and Virgil's poetry, and all the other things you have in mind and I have in mind, to which the name has been by tradition applied, are poetry, and that anything else is poetry which is naturally akin to those works. The difference between good and bad poetry is another matter.

Roughly speaking, in discussion we are accustomed to divide works of literary expression into poetry, into verse and into prose. The distinction between poetry and verse, the line of demarcation, is not always clear, and the two are often mingled in one work. The line between verse and prose is not always so clear as it might be, the line between poetry and prose is even a shadowy line, like the line between day and night, which nevertheless exists ; they are there, though we cannot exactly delimit their frontiers. Our subject this afternoon has to do with poetry.

How are we to begin ? If you proceed on the ordinary lines of any investigator who wishes to discover the properties of a particular class of objects, you will assemble in your minds all the works which you can recollect which fall by common consent into this classification of works of poetry. You will put them together, and you will see what qualities they have in common. I cannot enter in detail into the matter now, but I believe that if you go through that process, if you assemble all these works, or a suitable number of them, if you put them together and watch for features that they all have in common, and that can consequently be regarded as distinguishing marks of this class of object, you will find : first of all, that poetry is invariably strongly rhythmic, that it is marked by a regularity, a recurrence, a repetitiveness of rhythm which is different from what we are accustomed to find in prose ; and, secondly, that there is present in anything that is commonly agreed to be poetry a very strong emotional character which is invariably in poetry and is not invariably in prose, is usually absent therefrom ; and that what we are content to call

verse has the rhythmic characteristic of poetry but
not its emotional content.

Wordsworth, you will remember, when defining
poetry in a commonly accepted but partial definition (it left out, as I shall leave out this afternoon,
the whole aspect of art), said that it was " the spontaneous overflow of powerful feelings that had
sprung from emotion recollected in tranquillity."
The word " recollected " should not be taken in
too narrow a sense. Sometimes in experience we
" remember " an actual episode of our past with
its associated feelings, sometimes we " recover "
the emotion in connection with something which
we have never contemplated before. Let us accept
Wordsworth's statement that poetry, leaving out
the matter of art, has sprung from emotion. Let us
bear this in mind, and, bearing it in mind (and you
will certainly find that any modern work which has
" lasted " will confirm this impression), let us
examine a few works of poetry with a view to
discovering what their Subjects are.

We hear to-day (and this fact was the origin of
these lectures) a good deal of controversy with regard to the " subject matter of poetry "—rather a
vague term, as we shall presently discover. We hear
on the one hand a demand that " new subjects "
should be treated, that poets should not be content
with " working over the old themes " ; we sometimes hear on the other hand the piping voices
of elderly gentlemen complaining that there is too
much revolutionary tendency abroad, and that
subjects are dealt with, things are mentioned, that are
not suitable for treatment by a poet. There is that

controversy; and I think we shall be assisted if, instead of merely generalising in the matter, we do actually take one or two concrete instances, examine the poems and discover what their subjects are.

The other day I sat down in front of a number of volumes of poetry with the intention of doing that. The first thing I discovered was that in a general way a very short poem was not the most useful thing to consider. In most of the best, the most celebrated short poems, the subject is extremely simple ; you get the spontaneous overflow of powerful feelings in connection with one particular object or view— a man longs for his love, or thinks of a dead friend, and beyond that you often get little. I found that more light would be thrown if poems of a larger compass were taken, poems which were soon seen to contain a greater variety of subject matter than short poems normally do. The first poem that I took—and I took it more or less by chance—was " The Scholar Gipsy," by Matthew Arnold, and I put it to myself : What is this poem about ? Well, I found that it was about several things, that it was not about only one thing ; that very patently it was not only, or even perhaps chiefly, about the subject which Arnold in the title has avowedly given as its subject. To some extent it is about the Scholar Gipsy. In an old work by Glanvil (who, had this Institution been in existence at that time, would certainly have been an ornament of it, a man of wide and curious learning), in that old book by Glanvil, Matthew Arnold found a reference to a graduate of the University of Oxford who grew tired, as others have grown before and since, of

6

the academic atmosphere, but who took the course, unusual in his day and in ours, of expressing his weariness by leaving the town and linking up for the rest of his life with a band of wandering gipsies. Years after he left, some friends of his met him : they entered into conversation with him : he expressed no regret for the step he had taken, but said that the secret of magic was known to his vagabond comrades and that he was learning their arts, and proposed, when he discovered them, to publish the results to the world, which he never did.

That is the story which Matthew Arnold found : that story is the origin of his poem : that is the figure he was contemplating : that is the subject which he named in the title of his work:

> The story of that Oxford scholar poor
> Of pregnant parts and quick inventive brain,
> Who, tir'd of knocking at Preferment's door,
>   One summer morn forsook
> His friends, and went to learn the Gipsy lore.

Certainly this, in a sense, is the subject of the Scholar Gipsy ; but proceed and you will find that a great deal is " dealt with " that is not the Scholar Gipsy ; that there are subordinate subjects. This time, as a matter of fact, they are more important than they often are, because of the poet's leisurely and discursive methods. The chief of them, perhaps, are the landscape round Oxford, which makes a background for the picture of the Scholar and his life among the gipsies, and the bewilderments and vicissitudes of modern life, the tone of which is contrasted with the Scholar Gipsy's " unclouded joy " in the atmosphere of an older age ; these are the chief—they might be multiplied.

A poem, in a sense, is about anything which is mentioned in the course of it ; whatever is mentioned you must take to be, so far as it goes, one of the subjects of a poem. But it will serve our purpose here if we single out only the principal subordinate subjects in this poem. There you have your second subject of the poem, or rather your second group of subjects. It was not only about this Scholar Gipsy ; it was also about the English landscape, and in some stanzas Arnold almost forgets his general theme and dwells loquaciously and at great length on the struggles of that age of doubt in which he lived and in which we still live.

But thirdly, the poem is " about " something which may arguably be considered as its subject matter above all ; it is about the emotion generated in the poet by the contemplation of his own situation and of its associated spectacles, and by him communicated to us with a minimum of explicit statement. The emotions in so long a poem as this are usually a complex of emotions, even on the surface. The poet felt and the reader feels a pure and tranquil joy at certain of the scenes that are reflected in the poem. Yet there is no doubt as to what are the predominating, the prevailing, the essential emotions that he is experiencing in it. We know the moment ; we have known it with its musical lament which expresses regret for the transience of things and the frustration of life. The Scholar Gipsy is stated in

8

terms to be one symbol of indisputable happiness and peace, but even his figure, known to have departed so long ago, adds to the sense of mortality. Even the " grave Tyrian trader " and the " merry Greek coaster," who enter in a stanza at the end, throw their weight really, when we have finished and are taking in a complete impression, into the same scale. They are bright images from a vanished past, from a vanished world. There is not a stanza, there is scarcely a phrase, which is not charged with the same feelings. " The line of festal light in Christ-Church hall " which the Gipsy saw from the hill was to Matthew Arnold, and must be to many of his readers, a picture suggesting happier years and regret for the passage of all mortal things.

So there is a rough analysis. You have the nominal subject, which is the first starting-off point, the thing that serves as a skeleton ; you have, secondly, the subordinate subjects which are mentioned at some length ; you have, thirdly, this last matter that I have referred to, which, in a sense, we can regard as the predominating subject of the poem, the poet's exhibition of the passage of things and of the mystery of this mortal life, the mystery to which Matthew Arnold, like many poets and unlike others, professed to have no solution, not even the vestige of a solution.

Take secondly Gray's " Elegy " : ask yourself, What is the subject of Gray's " Elegy " ? You may speak superficially like the people who go about and say, " Why doesn't somebody write a poem about wireless telephony ? " or " I have written a poem

about wireless telephony," or " It is impossible
to write a poem about wireless telephony." If you
take this superficial view you will say that this is a
poem about the churchyard at Stoke Poges. Well,
Gray calls the poem an " Elegy written in a Country
Churchyard." There then is your starting-off point,
there is the thing that provides your skeleton—he
catalogues a considerable number of the graves.
But you must stop there, and just as you proceeded
from that one thing to others with Matthew Arnold's
" Scholar Gipsy," so, when you sit down to ask
yourself what Gray's " Elegy " is about, you will
very speedily discover that it is about other things
besides the churchyard which is at Stoke Poges.
It is about the " lowing herd " that is " winding
o'er the lea " : it is about the " swallow twitt'ring
from the straw-built shed " : it is about all sorts of
human lives, both proud and humble, which are
passed in review by the poet, and which get their
little meed of description and comment. And here
again, when you have catalogued all the objects
specifically named and the episodes specifically
dealt with in the poem, you will find that, once more,
there is a third thing that the poem is about, not so
liberally stated by Gray as it was by Matthew
Arnold, who is very frank in this regard, but nevertheless obviously there. It is about the feelings that
Thomas Gray had, whether in Stoke Poges churchyard, or even in his own study or in any of the
churchyards of the world, in the face of human
destiny, a feeling most intensely latent in the phrase :
" the paths of glory lead but to the grave."
    There, ladies and gentlemen, I have perhaps

taken two poems that are rather similar in character, but had the poet's emotion in the " Elegy in the Country Churchyard " been of another kind, these main groups of subject would have remained the same in number. The third poem I may take is, so far as mood is concerned, different from either of those—I refer to Francis Thompson's " Hound of Heaven " (I have deliberately taken three well-known poems of a considerable length). There once more (for the fashion of calling a work of literature by a name which had no reference to the contents whatever had not then developed) you have a poem which is " about " something stated in the title. It is about the Hound of Heaven, an image representing the persistent chase of God in the human soul, the never-failing voice of conscience, and in the end the surrender of the soul to what is emblematised by a hound. But here again you will find your subordinate subjects. The varied experiences of an average life are sketched in stanza after stanza, and you have a very notable and even magnificent picture, a dream picture of heaven. And there, once more, having exhausted that, you come to the third subject—and I think the word " subject " can truly be applied to it—the poet's emotion. His mood is different, his feelings are different feelings from those which we observe in those other two poems. His conscience and his consciousness also are in face of the immense doubt ; he also is aware of eternity behind time ; but his contemplation of all human vicissitudes leaves him in the peace, in the joyful peace, of a surrender to faith. It is a different mood, but the important thing is that there, dominating everything, as one of the subjects, is the poet's emotion in the presence of a particular spectacle or a particular series of spectacles.

You may examine as many works as you like. The shorter the poem the purer the emotion, the less profuse the objects mentioned ; but you will come to the conclusion that the main emotion, the dominating emotion, is the principal thing, that all roads lead to it, and you will also come to the conclusion that the other subjects, though subsidiary to that emotion, are in proportion to the length of the works. And you will also in the end perceive, from whatever period you draw your examples, that that main subject, the poet's emotion, is not notably changed from one age to another, or from one generation to another. This produces (and as I said I shall dwell particularly on change, the possibility of changing, etc., in our own time, next week) that air of commonplaceness, that degree of traditionalism which is not observable to the same extent in any other spheres of literature, which we cannot but notice in poetry, and which appears to give many people so much offence, and to be the cause of so much irritation and complaint. In so far as it is true that the emotion of the poet is, as it were, the principal subject of any poem, to that extent innovation is not possible. The chief emotions of mankind are the same in all parts of the world where man exists, and they have been the same, so far as we are able to discover, in all ages where man, capable of composition, has composed. You have your emotions of love linked up with the perception of the beautiful, whether in people or in things : you have your fear, your hatred—which is for the opposite of something you love, something different from the thing loved : you have the few emotions which we refer to in our common speech by names as ordinary and as ancient as that, and those emotions which are most powerful in us are the emotions which would have been catalogued (and have been to some extent by Aristotle and by the poets of his era) as the governing emotions of humanity. You will find precisely these few emotions in any poem which has come down to us from any ancient time or from any distant country.

This makes, so far as it goes, for a community in all poetry. The lament over Lesbia's sparrow resembles the lament over Juliet's owl, and an elegy on Mr. Jones has only in one regard a different subject from an elegy on Mr. Smith. A poem on the beauty of an aeroplane—a gliding thing—is not different from a poem on the beauty of a ship—another moving thing, because, all other parallelisms apart, it is about, in the first instance, the feelings that we have when we see a vehicle, the form of which appeals to us, the motion of which appeals to us, passing across the landscape.

And, apart from that community, the community which exists, so far as the emotional subject is concerned, there is a likeness, to a large extent, in the other groups, in the nominal subject and the subordinate subjects that are incidentally dealt with in the course of a poem. Here again, if once more you cast your mind backward, this time not over the products of literature but over human lives, this admission will not be found to be surprising. In many of the aspects of life, change comes rapidly, and in some periods, as for instance our own, with exceptional multiplicity and speed. There are very many differences—the smallest child in the street knows them—between our own age and the age in which Homer wrote. Everything that we use which the Greeks had is of a different shape ; we use a great many objects of which they did not know : we have made discoveries which were entirely unguessed by them : we wear clothes, we travel in vessels, we employ instruments which are different from theirs. But in spite of all that change, when you are dealing not with the subject matter of economic life and of ordinary prose—the Bradshaw Time-table to take an extreme example—when you are dealing, not with that but with the subject matter of poetry, with the things that generate those strong emotions which, as we have agreed, are an invariable mark of poetry, you will discover that those things which directly cause the deepest emotions we know in ourselves are in a general way the things, the experiences, the events or human relations, which caused their deepest emotions in the ancient Greeks, in the ancient Romans, in any people you care to choose, however remote in time. You can construct a rough outline of a human life embodying all the main episodes, the main incidents with which the majority of our deepest emotional experiences are connected ; and if you make such an outline, and if you put down the things that have most powerfully, most abidingly moved yourself, and which to your knowledge most powerfully move people of your time, you will find that such an outline of a life would apply as truly, as well to an ancient life as to your own, that not a word of it need be altered if you were attempting to describe the emotional life of a Greek. We are born, we pass through a period of childhood, on which we all look back with a certain sentiment, we reach maturity, we probably fall in love, we probably get married, we have relations with our particular friends, and others with our parents, and others with our husbands or wives, and others with our children ; we then spend a certain number of years on this earth looking forward to the certainty of death, either depressed by the shortness of life, or courageously attempting to keep our courage up and our energies active in spite of the conditions under which we live. And whenever at moments we are by ourselves, detached from the ordinary everyday incidents of life, or under a night sky looking at the stars, we return to this wonder of our existence, to the riddle of what was before our birth and what will be after our death, to the mystery of the Power that so strangely governs our destinies. There, in some such brief outline as that, you can contain all the principal events, all the principal experiences which produce the most powerful human emotions, and that outline, as I said, is an outline which includes nothing peculiar to our own time, nothing that humanly speaking we can call either new or old. So just as that first fact made for a traditionalism, a perpetuity, a recurrence with regard to the emotional subject, there are other facts that we cannot get away from, and that make, to a large extent, for repetition, for traditionalism, as some would call it for monotony, in the subjects of poetry of the first and of the second group.

But I will go further : not only are the principal events in our lives as human beings, in our relations with the universe and with our fellows, in broad outline the same from generation to generation, but to a large extent the physical landscape around us, like the moral landscape, remains unchanged. New elements may and do come into the landscape. Sometimes we may see such a new thing in a powerful light. Sometimes something which was unknown to any other generation but our own may be in our presence when we are feeling powerfully moved, may open like a window into infinity, may be envisaged as part of a scene which is the natural accessory or background to the story we are narrating, or may come into our mind as an apt image to symbolise something which we wish to symbolise. But in a general way, it is not strange that even in the detail of poetry—which is not primarily giving information, which is not primarily satisfying intellectual curiosity, but which is simply treating naturally of those deep human emotions—it is not strange that, even in point of detail and so far as regards the most subordinate objects " mentioned," we should observe a good deal of continuity from generation to generation, a good deal in common between the poems, say, of Virgil's age and the poems of our own. For although in Virgil's day this building did not exist, the chances are that if we should happen to have some rare experience it won't take place here : if we associate with one of our deepest emotional experiences any particular physical object, it won't be these benches. For why? This building takes up so very little space in the world. To begin with, in any landscape almost, the sky occupies one half. You look there, you see the sky, the earth, the fields (however some of them by cultivation may be changed in certain aspects), the trees, the sea, the winds, the seasons, the heavenly bodies. All these large things are unchanged by anything that we do, and from a merely statistical point of view, it is quite obvious that when we are describing any particular experience that is not selected as unusual, but only for its emotional depth, we shall most often naturally recall in connection with it one of these major objects that has always arrested the eye rather than any other object that is peculiar to our own time. So there even with regard to subordinate objects ; the objects you will find mentioned in Gray's " Elegy," which were tombstones, and the fates of kings and the humbleness of the poor, the trees and cattle and swallows twittering in their nests, all those things might just as well have been mentioned by an ancient, and if one of our own contemporaries happened to be contemplating human mortality—which is one of those things that do most profoundly move every one of us—it would very likely come natural to him to mention precisely those objects that Gray mentioned, and possibly to mention no others.

Well, ladies and gentlemen, I have here, I find, a quotation from Carlyle which rather emphasises what I have just been saying as to the perpetuity of subject in poetry, and of the classes of subject in poetry. Carlyle in that essay says :

Does Homer interest us now because he wrote of what passed beyond his native Greece and two centuries before he was born ; or because he wrote what passed in God's world, and in the heart of man, which is the same after thirty centuries ?

My point goes a little further than Carlyle's, because to a large extent I have been suggesting that Homer actually did not write of what passed in his native Greece two centuries before he was born in so far as those things were peculiar to his native Greece, but actually wrote when at his heights of those major things which are not peculiar to any age. On the other hand—and here we are approaching the other side of the subject, the subject of innovation, of development, of growth, which I propose to deal with next week—Wordsworth (in a passage which I should like always to see bracketed with that other, as that other with this), said :

It is the honourable characteristic of poetry that its materials are to be found in every subject which can interest the human mind. The evidence of this fact is to be sought, not in the writings of critics, but in those of the poets themselves.

Next week, having emphasised this week the natural, the necessary, the inevitable (whatever you may feel about it) element of traditionalism in the subjects, in all classes of the subjects of poetry, I shall endeavour to expand, to expound, and to illustrate what I believe to be the profound truth of Wordsworth's sentences which I have just quoted.

SUBJECT IN POETRY

I shall argue that there is nothing which cannot be the serious and avowed subject of poetry, nothing, no object, no experience, no implement which cannot be mentioned, nothing which may not occur in the course of, which may not inspire, a good poem.

SUBJECT IN POETRY

II

LADIES and Gentlemen, you will remember
that last week I considered what was the
nature of the subject of poetry, of the poetry
that we have inherited, and I examined certain
specified poems with a view to analysing roughly
their content.

We found that, roughly speaking, we should
divide it into three parts: There was first of all the
avowed subject, the subject which supplied the
whole outline of the poem, the outline or at least the
starting-point. There was, secondly, a number, vary-
ing according to the nature and length of the work,
of subordinate subjects coming down to things that
were merely mentioned, either as parts of a background, or as images. And thirdly, we found that
we had—and it is impossible not to consider that a
part of the subject of poetry—we had the emotion
which the poet felt and which he was distinctly
writing about as much as he was writing about the
nominal subject of his work.

We then discovered by a very rapid survey, a con-
spectus of the works of the past, that so far as the
emotion was concerned, little change could be recorded, and that so far as those other objects, those
objects which were mentioned or which were
avowedly taken as the themes for poems, were concerned, there was remarkably little change throughout recorded history. That is to say, that to-day in

many instances the avowed themes of the poems
that people write are precisely the same as were
taken two or three thousand years ago, and, in a large
measure, the actual imagery that you come upon in
the course of your reading of acknowledged good
poetry of our day, is exactly the same as we might
find in corresponding poems of Shakespeare's
day.

I then proceeded, you may remember, to argue
that that was natural and inevitable ; that owing
to the very nature of poetry, springing as it does
from, and representing, our profoundest emotions,
it was inevitable that certain emotions experienced
in human life should continually be represented,
and also that, in view of the evidence of the physical
world around us, that changes so little from generation to generation, it was not strange that, even with
regard to the subordinate matters dealt with in
poetry, change should not be very violent or very
frequent.

But I did not leave it at that. Although I had
emphasised in quite a detached way what you might
call the conservative, the traditional, the perpetual,
the recurrent elements in poetry, so far as the content is concerned, although I had been laying stress
upon these, saying that they were there and moreover that it was quite inevitable that in genuine
poetry they should be there, I did conclude by
quoting some sentences by Wordsworth to the effect
that there was no subject in the world which could
not be properly dealt with in poetry if the poet was
feeling in the right frame of mind about it. I said
that that was my opinion, and that I should spend

this afternoon in endeavouring, so far as I could, to expand my view on that a little.

We will consider, therefore, to-day chiefly this matter of the introduction of new subjects into poetry, the taking of new themes, the mentioning of objects not familiar to our predecessors. We do hear around us continually (and for that reason I think it was worth while dealing with this matter) two kinds of comment on this question. We do get from persons of a conservative frame of mind complaints that the revolutionary young are introducing into their works subjects which are unfit for poetry, which are essentially unpoetical, and are mentioning things about which we would rather not be reminded ; and we do get, on the other hand, persons who are tired of what I believe to be the inevitable traditional elements—there are times when most of us feel like that perhaps—and who argue that anyone who wishes to prove himself an artist must at once tackle what they call " the host of new subjects " with which our world is full.

Well, look again very briefly—we have no time to enter into much detail—look again at that body of poetry which we have inherited from the past, and to which I commended your attention last week. If you look at it, ruling out that large element of continuity, of repetition, of almost monotony, which, as I said, was the first thing that would strike your notice, if you will leave that out and watch only for the intervention of elements which, although not new to our time, were new to the poets when they first wrote, you will find throughout history in every generation when poetry was not merely an academic confection of verses—composed as boys in public schools compose Latin verses, imitating someone else cold-bloodedly and in terms refusing to write of or mention anything that their predecessors have not mentioned—in any age when poetry has been alive, that, however cautiously, using whatever filter, the poets have invariably introduced into their works other new characteristics (there always are as well modulations of metre and what not), words and terms, subjects and objects, which were not employed by their immediate or by their remoter predecessors. Look at it the other way : think of any specific object, any object of our world that exists now, and which did not exist, say, six hundred years ago. The longer it has existed, the more certainly you will find that it has been incorporated into our poetry and invested with that indefinable aura with which great poetry always invests anything which it mentions.

Take, to go back a long way, modern weapons, guns and cannons. There can be no doubt whatever that when these implements were first introduced in, I suppose, the fourteenth century, persons who were then writing verses, mostly at that date amorous, thought that these weapons were extremely unpicturesque, that they were absolutely unsuited to poetry, that they made a great noise and a great smell and were very ugly, compared with the bows and arrows to which they had been accustomed before. There happened to be, immediately after that, a considerable lacuna in our poetry, a period during which little was written except religious verses ; but no sooner was it revived than

we find that these innovations (which were just as
novel to that day as the motor-car is to ours) were
seized upon, were incorporated, were embodied in
poetry, and by the time you get to Milton, you find
that great poet actually including artillery in his
heavenly battles. Talk about heavenly battles and
artillery !—the thing has now become so universally
accepted as a thing that can be mentioned, as much
as the sea or a cloud, that we actually have for the
thunder a dead phrase, " heaven's artillery," which
only cannot be used, not because there is too much
novelty about it, but because it is too stale.

Take a second instance, the mechanical vehicles
propelled by steam power, new things a hundred
and twenty or a hundred years ago, the steamships,
the trains, and a little later the ironclads. We all
know—everybody who has ever read a few books of
the period must know—that when those things came
into our world, they were not only regarded by the
ordinary citizen as extremely noisy and dirty things
(which in a large measure they still are), but they
were thought of as quite irredeemably ugly and most
certainly as things that could not conceivably be
mentioned in a sonnet. To-day there is nothing
astonishing whatever in a man taking a man-o'-war
or even a train as a subject of a poem. Having seen
one effective poem on such a subject, we are at once
used to it, and are no longer surprised if other people
write a hundred. The early view of the train was
very much what the view of the motor-car in 1900
was : that it was nothing but a mechanical com-
pilation of mechanical parts that was being used
for a material purpose, a thing upon which a poet

should turn his back, and from which it was not
conceivable that he should derive æsthetic sensa-
tions. That was the early view, but half-way through
the Victorian age the train slowly began puffing
its way into literature. You will find in almost
all your great Victorian poets that they approached
it gradually. The first thing that struck them about
it, that actually moved them, was usually a vision
in the distance from a hill-top of the little row of
puffs of white smoke that came out of the funnel of
a train in the middle of a placid sunlit expanse of
land ; probably most of the early appearances of
the locomotive in poetry were made in that manner.
Little by little the object became quite commonplace
until even the most recondite, the most obdurate of
poets were liable to introduce the train—that abomin-
able machine that was so unæsthetic—into verse. Over
the most Arcadian poetry the smoke of it trails ; now-
adays telegraph posts, which are beautiful things,
come in with it ; and by the time we get to the late
John Davidson, we actually have, I think, what is the
first poem of any merit entirely devoted to the subject :

> Crash under bridges,
> Flash over ridges
> And vault the downs ;
> The road is straight
> Nor stile, nor gate ;
> For milestones—towns !
>
> Voluminous, vanishing white,
> The steam plume trails ;
> Parallel streaks of light,
> The polished rails.

Hark ! hark ! hark !
It screams and cleaves the dark,
And the subterranean night
Is gilt with smoky light ;
Then out again apace
It runs its thundering race.

There, although you have not a masterpiece, you have the outline of a thing which is essentially a poem, a thing which is derived, not from any mere desire to write about a train, but from an æsthetic sensation, an emotional experience, actually felt, by a man who was at last ready, without bias, without prejudice, to expose himself, as it were, to the light that came from the train.

Look at any collection of nineteenth-century poetry and you will find here and there that things are mentioned which could not have appeared in previous centuries. In Browning's " Meeting at Night " you find the lines :

A tap at the pane, the quick sharp scratch
And blue spurt of a lighted match.

The match now appears no odder to us than the pane ; but the match was novel in Browning's day, and time was when there were no panes. Canon Beeching's poem about " coasting " on a bicycle was almost contemporaneous with the bicycle's appearance on our roads. In Sir Henry Newbolt you come upon :

He watch'd the liner's stern ploughing the foam,
He felt her trembling speed, and the thrash of her
screw.

SUBJECT IN POETRY

In Mr. Bridges you find :

> An engine pants and hums
> In the farm hard by :
> Its lowering smoke is lost
> In the lowering sky.

Liner and engine are encountered now with as little surprise as though they had been coeval with foam and farm.

Similarly we shall find, undoubtedly, in our own generation, that everything else which has come into our lives, in our own day, every new thing, not only things that we rapidly perceive to have a conventional beauty of line, but even things that we continue to think intrinsically ugly, will be absorbed, as it were, into the corpus of English poetry.

All, or almost all, of the most hideous devices of modern warfare were thus brought into our poetic literature during the late war. There was a time (we can all remember it, not more than fifteen or twenty years ago) when the sky-scrapers of New York were almost universally regarded, I won't say with disapproval, but with horror. It was quite common form, when you were mentioning those buildings, to refer to them as though they were the most repulsive constructions that man's ingenuity had ever hit upon. We do not find that now : even had we not discovered (I am not entering now into the general question of the desirability of higher buildings for London) that those things actually had externally, the best of them, the most magnificent architectural qualities, it would have been because they were so dominating or because they were for so important a community that they had been introduced, ugly or beautiful, or for some other reason. They would have come in : to some they would have represented home when they were away : to others, travelling from this side, those things must necessarily be associated with the emotions that any man must sustain when he first approaches a new continent after a long voyage across an ocean ; they would have been associated naturally with a large number of human dramas which had taken place in their shadow ; and at worst, at lowest, there are times, there are seasons, when even the ugliest of objects, if conspicuous, must impress us and strike us as having a quality of physical beauty. Almost any town viewed from outside is quite conventionally beautiful at dawn, and again at twilight, and again at night, when it is lit up by lights. From those tall buildings you get an arrangement, an impression, of civic lights such as you get from no other buildings in the world at night. I say, therefore, that it was quite inevitable that those things should be introduced into literature, and now we have become quite accustomed to it ; and if you are reading any modern American verses, you are never surprised if a man happens to mention, or even take as his ostensible main theme, a building forty storeys high.

Take the aeroplanes again : there again, when they first went up, most of us looked at them quite cold-bloodedly : all that we saw was a mechanical device that had overcome the difficulty of lifting a body heavier than air and moving it through the air ; our first impression was that aeroplanes looked rather like trams going about the sky.

SUBJECT IN POETRY

For some little while, so far as I know, the aeroplane did evade English verse, at any rate, good English verse ; once or twice it may have come in, just as the train came in in the beginning, incidentally, just flying about in the background, rather like a bird taking short flights at first. But in a very few years there were produced (and I propose reading a couple of them) quite a number of extremely good poems that were not only about aeroplanes incidentally, but actually took aeroplanes as their avowed subjects.

I have here two poems about aeroplanes, or at any rate aeroplaning, written during the war—neither of them, I may incidentally remark, which is interesting, by a poet of very conspicuous reputation ; one of them, in fact, by a young man who was killed almost immediately after writing it. I would like with your permission to read them, although the first of them is rather long.

The first is very much more closely devoted to the aeroplane and its details than the second. It is called " On the Wings of the Morning," and is by a flying officer of the name of Jeffery Day :

A sudden roar, a mighty rushing sound,
    a jolt or two, a smoothly sliding rise,
a tumbled blur of disappearing ground,
    and then all sense of motion slowly dies.
        Quiet and calm, the earth slips past below,
        as underneath a bridge still waters flow.

My turning wing inclines towards the ground ;
    the ground itself glides up with graceful swing

and at the plane's far tip twirls slowly round,
    then drops from sight again beneath the wing
      to slip away serenely as before,
    a cubist-patterned carpet on the floor.

Hills gently sink and valleys gently fill.
    The flattened fields grow ludicrously small ;
slowly they pass beneath and slower still
    until they hardly seem to move at all.
      Then suddenly they disappear from sight,
      hidden by fleeting wisps of faded white.

The wing-tips, faint and dripping, dimly show,
    blurred by the wreaths of mist that intervene.
Weird, half-seen shadows flicker to and fro
    across the pallid fog-bank's blinding screen.
      At last the choking mists release their hold,
      and all the world is silver, blue, and gold.

The air is clear, more clear than sparkling wine ;
    compared with this, wine is a turgid brew.
The far horizon makes a clean-cut line
    between the silver and the depthless blue.
      Out of the snow-white level reared on high
      glittering hills surge up to meet the sky.

Outside the wind-screen's shelter gales may race :
    but in the seat a cool and gentle breeze
blows steadily upon my grateful face.
    As I sit motionless and at my ease,
      contented just to loiter in the sun
      and gaze around me till the day is done.

SUBJECT IN POETRY

And so I sit, half sleeping, half awake,
  dreaming a happy dream of golden days,
until at last, with a reluctant shake
    I rouse myself, and with a lingering gaze
      at all the splendour of the shining plain
      make ready to come down to earth again.

The engine stops : a pleasant silence reigns—
  silence, not broken, but intensified
by the soft, sleepy wires' insistent strains,
    that rise and fall, as with a sweeping glide
      I slither down the well-oiled sides of space,
      towards a lower, less enchanted place.

The clouds draw nearer, changing as they come.
  Now, like a flash, fog grips me by the throat.
Down goes the nose : at once the wires' low hum
    begins to rise in volume and in note,
      till, as I hurtle from the choking cloud
      it swells into a scream, high-pitched, and loud.

The scattered hues and shades of green and brown
  fashion themselves into the land I know,
turning and twisting, as I spiral down
    towards the landing-ground ; till, skimming low,
      I glide with slackening speed across the ground,
      and come to rest with lightly grating sound.

There is one. I will make some comments on it a
little later, because there are some interesting points
to be noted.

Here is another, " Nox Mortis," by another flying
officer, a man named Paul Bewsher :

The afternoon
    Flutters and dies :
The fairy moon
    Burns in the skies
As they grow darker, and the first stars shine
On Night's rich mantle—purple like warm wine.

On each white road
    Begins to crawl
The heavy toad :
    The night-birds call,
And round the trees the swift bats flit and wheel,
While from the barns the rats begin to steal.

So now must I,
    Bird of the night,
Towards the sky
    Make wheeling flight,
And bear my poison o'er the gloomy land,
And let it loose with hard unsparing hand.

The chafers boom
    With whirring wings,
And haunt the gloom
    Which twilight brings—
So in nocturnal travel do I wail
As through the night the wingèd engines sail.

Death, Grief, and Pain
    Are what I give.
O that the slain
    Might live—might live !
I know them not, for I have blindly killed,
And nameless hearts with nameless sorrow filled.

SUBJECT IN POETRY

Thrice cursèd War
Which bids that I
Such death should pour
Down from the sky.
O, Star of Peace, rise swiftly in the East
That from such slaying men may be released.

And so you see that everything comes in, and when
it has come in genuinely as the aeroplane has come
in there, it does not at all appear with a shock.
Everything arrives, mechanical discoveries, changes
in the fashion of things, new scientific speculations, new psychological theories. Freud will leave
his mark on poetry as Darwin did. But there are
several reservations, several qualifications to be
entered when one makes this statement. The first
is, as I said last week, that if we merely let ourselves alone (be as receptive as you like, but be
genuine, not forcing, not making things up, not
chasing after the new for the sake of the new), the
traditional element is bound to be there, as it is
bound to be dominant.

You will find that there have been in our time a
large number of attempts on the part of persons,
usually not intended to be poets at all, to write poems
about new things which have come into the world
simply because nobody has done so before. " Here,"
they will say—and there are people who encourage
them—" here is a subject that never was tackled
yet ; let us tackle it and we shall not only get credit
ourselves, but we shall enlarge the scope of poetry."
A man will cold-bloodedly go down to, say, Picca-
dilly Circus and inform us of what he sees. But if his

primary motive is merely to write about something new, you will invariably find that he fails, and that he fails in one of two ways. Either he gives you, being totally oblivious of the necessity of that emotional element in poetry that is always agreed to be at the back of it, a well-meant but prosaic statement that may, or may not, be exciting, that certainly did not need to be in verse and does not affect you in such a manner that you want to go back to it afterwards ; either that, or else we feel that there is a tone of strenuosity about the poetry which is different from what we have learned to expect. Aware that emotion must be expressed, the gentleman will invent emotions that he does not actually feel ; and when you do that you invariably tend to force the pace and to exaggerate, you use strong language and you throw about your imagery in a very violent way. You screw things up, you pretend to see things and to hear things very much more strongly than you do, and the result is boredom on the part of the reader. Even in a certain number of good compositions you can see the result of theorising a little too much. For example, in Mr. Kipling's " McAndrew's Hymn." That poem to me has always been a mixture. I think Mr. Kipling is a very good poet, but this has always appeared to me to be a mixture between a good poem about a ship's engines and a man, and a bad one. Mr. Kipling did indubitably feel genuine emotions at the sight of what goes on in the engine-room, both with the men and with the engines, which might at any moment appear very beautiful in their strength to any poet who was in a receptive mood ; but he was

34

determined to drag in as much of the novelty of the thing as he could. The result is a good deal of talk about cranks, pistons, and what not, that strikes the reader as a little false, and really conveys nothing at all to him, for he does not know a piston from whatever the other things in an engine-room are.

This very peculiar fault in theory is to be freely found in the works of John Davidson, from whom I quoted just now the poem about the train. John Davidson was a man with scientific interests and a man of great originality, but he handicapped himself considerably by his deliberate search for new subjects. He wrote poems which are very affecting and beautiful and musical, mostly about subjects like the dawn and deer-hunting and things of that kind, but he also wrote as profusely as he could about every possible kind of thing that had not been written about before, and in the end, having tackled and dealt with every other subject, he determined to sit down and write a poem, a serious poem, about the Crystal Palace. Well, it is quite conceivable, it is quite possible, that a man might write a very good poem about the Crystal Palace : he might suddenly find the Crystal Palace in the background of some experience, or he might suddenly see the Crystal Palace in a particular light as a thing of beauty, or he might see it as a monument of the dead (which it is as truly as anything that has been found in the tombs of the Pharaohs) ; a man might have all sorts of emotional experiences in the Crystal Palace, but the point was that Davidson had not had those, but that he felt he would like to write a poem on the theme. The result was that almost as soon as

35

he started he realis:d the impossible situation and began to make jokes about it.

Well, then, the second thing which must qualify our conviction that anything can be dealt with in poetry is, that it has to be felt. We must be chosen by our subjects, not choose them ; write because we feel like writing, not because we have a theory that this, that, or the other can no longer be ignored by poets.

And the third qualification is this : that when a new theme actually does present itself in the right way, the traditional elements still intrude themselves. When men do deal with what is called " a new subject," you will usually find that when you sit down to consider the work, if it is a good work, if it is a work that you feel appeals to you and will go on appealing to you, that it really is not principally about the new subject at all. Take, for example, those two other poems that I read to you just now. They both are by practical aeroplanists, and they both describe, or at any rate, both have as their nominal subject, flying. The first one actually does enter with some detail into what goes on physically during a flight ; when you look for the real elements of novelty in the next you will find that beyond the mention of the flying machine, there is really very little that is new at all. The appeal of the thing rests in something quite old, something that could have been associated with emotion on a journey of some other kind, in some other vehicle, and little pain is taken to expand precisely—to mention even precisely—those qualities, those parts which differentiate an aeroplane from anything else.

SUBJECT IN POETRY

We know (or rather, I do not know, but some of you will know) scientifically all sorts of things about aeroplanes, things which, if you were sitting down to write an article for the Encyclopædia, would be extremely numerous and no doubt extremely interesting and extremely novel, things that were not known thirty or forty years ago. Here is a new construction dependent on all sorts of mysterious processes, but none of them is mentioned in these two poems. You will find that through natural association, a few things do creep in ; you will find a reference to " wing-tips," (although there again the *word* is not new), and to various other things, parts of an aeroplane, which are, as it were, new things in literature. Even so, those things only come in incidentally. What one of those poems is about really is the light, the sun, the landscape, the sensation that one gets through rapid motion, and, underneath the surface, the feeling of the joy and the mystery of life, which a man might have had in a Greek ship as much as this man in an aeroplane, although not precisely from the same angle. That was one of them. The other really scarcely mentions the aeroplane at all, but is about the mystery of human destiny, the ancient problem of why it was that we are here struggling against each other and compelled to inflict evil upon each other : this is its chief theme, it is a poem of pity.

What you find there you will find in any genuine poem, I think, whatever its ostensible subject, even if one should get a poem about broadcasting, or about the latest thing that came into the papers. I imagine there was a time when people

would have been shocked, some people, if they had
been told that a man would write a poem about a
malaria microbe : there were other people, no doubt,
who, had they been told that a man was going to
write a poem about the malaria microbe, would have
been delighted and would have thrown up their
caps because they expected to find something absolutely new in literature. Well, there was such a poem :
it was written by Sir Ronald Ross, the man who
actually got hold of this microbe. But when he wrote
it, it was not about the differences between malaria
microbes and other microbes : it was not about
microbes at all. The microbes are no more important
than the " French copper coins " in Coventry Patmore's " The Toys," which also, though their like
had existed for centuries, had probably never been
introduced into poetry before. Its opening words give
the key to it :

> This day relenting God
> Hath put within my hand
> A wondrous thing.

There you find that the novel thing is really only a
channel for the communication of the ancient emotions ; and, do what you like, you will find that that
happens.

There is a poem by a younger poet, Rupert Brooke,
about dining-room tea, which is not a mechanical
invention, but may be regarded as a thing which
was, at any rate, an invention of the nineteenth
century in the social way. He wrote a poem about a
tea-party, but what did he give ? He did not convey

information about tea or about teapots ; what he did do was to write a poem in which he suddenly visualises the whole proceedings stopping, in which he suddenly sees the eternal behind the temporal, in which he suddenly sees the particular in the light of the universal, and he says :

> I saw the marble cup, the tea
> Hung on the air an amber stream. . .

That is, I think, universally true. So true is it that we may almost at first sight beware of a poem which is demonstratively and in great profusion of detail about a subject which is new to poetry. It is quite, I think, irrefutably true that this is bound to happen, that as you go from prose into poetry, so the element of information, this element of novelty, tends to diminish, so you get nearer to that area of the great commonplaces on which we human beings of all generations meet.

I might illustrate this by taking this very audience, this very building in which we are sitting now, The Royal Institution. I do not know if there has ever been written a poem about The Royal Institution, but suppose for a moment that this theatre were dealt with in the ordinary prose mood. A man would sit down and he would describe this hall ; he would probably mention the benches and that there were some ladies sitting up there, and that there was a desk here with an inkpot on it : that there was a water-bottle here, of rather an old pattern, and that it looked as though it might be of some value ; and then the form of the lights, the clock with a wooden

39

rim, and so on. Well, your next stage, which is hardly
a stage at all, is the stage towards verse, verse which
is not written in the poetic temper. There you may
convey as many statements as you like, although
conveying the same statements in verse usually makes
them look comic :

Here in the Institution Royal I stand. . .

(That, of course, is well marked ; it is a very good
thing if you can invert like that)

Enormous multitudes* on either hand,
The water-bottle is upon the desk,
It isn't useful, but still it's picturesque.

I haven't made the last line scan (I could make it scan
if I worked on it a little). But did I by any chance
write a poem, and not only a poem but a good one,
about this audience, do you think for a moment that
these objects would come in ? No, certain selected
ones would come in, which had associated themselves with the emotion I was feeling, certain things
which were for the time being united to me : I
should get certain emotions, but the poem, when
produced, would not be really or chiefly about The
Royal Institution at all. Something would suddenly
" hang one up " here ; either the lighting, or else
the physical beauty of your faces ; or one might
suddenly realise that here, sitting on these benches,
were immortal spirits clothed in fading flesh, and
one might in that manner, through this building as

* There were about forty people in the theatre, which is capable
of holding six or seven hundred.

40

SUBJECT IN POETRY

In the "Ancient Mariner," as printed in the "Lyrical Ballads," occurred the familiar lines :

> The fair breeze blew, the white foam flew,
> The furrow *followed* free.

Later, in "Sibylline Leaves," the second line was printed thus :

> The furrow *stream'd off* free.

And Coleridge appended to the revised line a note :

> In the former editions the line was "The furrow followed free." But I had not been long on board a ship before I perceived that this was the image as seen by a spectator from the shore, or from another vessel. From the ship itself the Wake appears like a brook flowing off from the stern.

Perfectly true, and truth of appearance at that. But supererogatory truth of fact lurks behind the change, none the less. For the Mariner, as Coleridge's intellect, hunting alone, perceived, was on the ship, not off it, and so should see the furrow streaming away, not following. But to obtrude that fact is to snap the spell—to take the Ancient Mariner from the mystery of his silent sea, and set him, an old sailor, at the stern of a boat. A line that is as inevitable as the nearing of the spectre bark itself was marred by a meticulous observance of irrelevant truth of fact. And eleven years later, with his unruly intellect in its place again, Coleridge restored the original reading.

Well, ladies and gentlemen, that suggests that even in so far as poetry incorporates new knowledge, or old knowledge for the matter of that, it does not necessarily incorporate it accurately. It does deal more, when it is mentioning these physical objects, with things as they appear to the poet when he is in a certain state of mind, a certain situation, and the chances are consequently that the differences between things—for in all there are very few qualities, even if you admit stickiness and shininess and so forth—will not be very much emphasised.

I conclude, therefore, ladies and gentlemen, that Wordsworth was quite right. Poetry gradually incorporates by means of the excitement generated in a man through his intellect or his senses, all the new subjects that come into this world, but it is not and it never will be a manual of information, and it is quite impossible, by merely taking pains, to incorporate new subjects faster than they allow themselves naturally to be incorporated. Step by step only, poetry will through the medium of poets glorify thing after thing that comes into the world, as it has glorified so many objects which have been familiar to all the ages of mankind.

I see that my time approaches, but before I stop I should just like to read to you two passages illustrating two sides of my argument dealing specifically with them. They are poems by living poets.

The first is a poem by Mr. De la Mare : he speaks of the process by which poetry does actually invest, as it can invest, even the most intractable material with beauty. The second is a passage which emphasises the necessary, the inevitable continuity in poetry.

SUBJECT IN POETRY

The first is a poem called " Farewell." This is
the process as Mr. Walter De la Mare sees it, a process which leaves the poet's posterity richer than
they would have been had his eyes not seen the thing
suddenly as beautiful, or used by him as a channel
with which to communicate something beautiful.
He is leaving his testament to us :

When I lie where shades of darkness
Shall no more assail my eyes,
Nor the rain make lamentation
    When the wind sighs ;
How will fare the world whose wonder
Was the very proof of me ?
Memory fades, must the remembered
    Perishing be ?

Oh, when this my dust surrenders
Hand, foot, lip, to dust again,
May those loved and loving faces
    Please other men !
May the rusting harvest hedgerows
Still the Traveller's Joy entwine,
And as happy children gather
    Posies once mine.

Look thy last on all things lovely
Every hour. Let no night
Seal thy sense in deathly slumber
    Till to delight
Thou have paid thy utmost blessing ;
Since that all things thou wouldst praise
Beauty took from those who loved them
    In other days.

There you have that truth that, through the
medium of poetry, the province of beauty is ex-
panded ; and there you have also, by the way, as
lovely a reflection of the finest poetic mood, un-
selfish and generous, as you could discover anywhere. And here you have an expansion, as I think
a very eloquent expansion, of certain passages in
my remarks last week. Mr. Bottomley—yes, I think
I had better qualify him—Mr. *Gordon* Bottomley
is suddenly thinking of that lost civilisation of
Atlantis, of which legend speaks, and wonders what
the poets wrote about who lived there before the
sea came over it ; and he comes to the conclusion
that they wrote about very much the same things as
we write about :

What poets sang in Atlantis ? Who can tell
The epics of Atlantis or their names ?
The sea hath its own murmurs, and sounds not
The secrets of its silences beneath,
And knows not any cadences enfolded
When the last bubbles of Atlantis broke
Among the quieting of its heaving floor.

O, years and tides and leagues and all their billows
Can alter not man's knowledge of men's hearts—
While trees and rocks and clouds include our
    being
We know the epics of Atlantis still :
A hero gave himself for lesser men,
Who first misunderstood and murdered him
And then misunderstood and worshipped him ;
A woman was lovely and men fought for her :

SUBJECT IN POETRY

Towns burnt for her, and men put men in bond-
    age,
But she put lengthier bondage on them all ;
A wanderer toiled among all the isles
That fleck this turning star of shifting sea,
Or lonely purgatories of the mind,
In longing for his home or his lost love.

Poetry is founded on the hearts of men :
Though in Nirvana or the heavenly courts
The principle of beauty shall persist,
Its body of poetry, as the body of man,
Is but a terrene form, a terrene use,
That swifter being will not loiter with ;
And, when mankind is dead, and the world cold,
Poetry's immortality will pass.

A NOTE ON THE EIGHTEENTH CENTURY

A HUNDRED years ago, when the greatest of the Romantics had already written most of their works for a public as yet small, substantial collections of the British Poets were the vogue. No gentleman's library was complete without a set, and neither editors, publishers, nor readers thought it strange that such sets should be mainly composed of verses written during the eighteenth century. A respectable critic of that time might or might not have troubled to inspect closely the obscure volumes of one Keats and one Shelley, but he would certainly be acquainted with the best compositions of Mr. Yalden, Mr. Duke and Mr. King, the elegant Dr. Langhorne and the unfortunate Richard Savage. When Wordsworth attacked his predecessors, nothing was seen in his disquisition but his ingratitude to a century which had taught him much, and his fortunate failure to conform to his own inadequate theories : nobody saw an omen. The eighteenth-century tradition was established ; Lord Byron, with all his eccentricities, was avowedly indebted to it ; and Mr. Rogers and Mr. Campbell, who would outlive all the young fantastics, were its worthy heirs. Keats dismissed the whole Georgian race in " Sleep and Poetry " :

Ah, dismal-soul'd !
The winds of heaven blew, the ocean roll'd
Its gathering waves—ye felt it not. The blue
Bared its eternal bosom, and the dew

Of summer night collected still to make
The morning precious : Beauty was awake !
Why were ye not awake ? But ye were dead
To things ye knew not of—were closely wed
To musty laws lined out with wretched rule
And compass vile ; so that ye taught a school
Of dolts to smooth, inlay, and clip, and fit,
Till, like the certain wands of Jacob's wit,
Their verses tallied. Easy was the task :
A thousand handicraftsmen wore the mask
Of Poesy. Ill-fated, impious race !
That blasphemed the bright Lyrist to his face,
And did not know it, no, they went about,
Holding a poor, decrepit standard out,
Mark'd with most flimsy mottoes, and in large
The name of one Boileau !

They did not know that this opinion would become
so general as to be regarded as a commonplace. Yet
it is scarcely an exaggeration to say that for generations past our critics and our cultivated public, looking backwards on our poetry, have been content to
leap the eighteenth century and concentrate almost
exclusively on the work of the Elizabethan and
Caroline eras. Pope and Dryden, who could not be
overlooked, have been underrated ; lip-service has
been paid to Prior and Gay ; for the others, only a
few such as Gray, Collins, Cowper and Goldsmith
have received consideration, and even those have
been regarded as chiefly interesting by virtue of
their position as " precursors of the Romantic Movement " or " heralds of the return to Nature." As a
fact they were the fine flower of the century ; and

the merits found in them were present in very many of their lesser contemporaries. In any event, those who lacked the qualities which appealed to the nineteenth century had virtues of their own. Occasionally a critic like Mr. Saintsbury, Mr. Gosse, Mr. Seccombe or Mr. Austin Dobson has called attention to this ; " The Hermit " and " The Choice," " The Hymn to the Naiads," " The Nocturnal Reverie," " Grongar Hill " and " The Rosciad " have all had their modern admirers. At rare intervals there has appeared a whole-hearted champion of the eighteenth century, such as Mr. Courthorpe, whose temperamental affinity to it made him put its poetry higher than any of the critics mentioned above would have put it, and who counter-attacked the Romantics with a list of charges as long as their own. I believe that the efforts of these and other men, exceptional in their freedom from literary fashion, have at last begun to restore our sense of proportion. Even they, however, who had to expend energy on justifying the right of eighteenth-century poetry to exist at all, were not able to devote themselves to the resuscitation of deserving minors. That work will be done, and its performance will synchronise with the growth of a more diffused inclination to see the eighteenth century as it was, to understand it and to do it—I speak only of its poetry—justice. It is now sufficiently removed from us. The necessity of fighting it was over long ago ; the prolongation of the war has been in part due to ignorance and misunderstanding, and in part merely mechanical, the unthinking perpetuation of a habit.

NOTE ON THE EIGHTEENTH CENTURY

I happen to live in a fragment of eighteenth-century London ; Middlesex it then was. Little lawns behind palings slope to the river in front ; the old brick houses have brick-walled gardens, trimly decorative doorways, occasionally a slender balcony ; and, inside, white-panelled rooms and shutters that fold back into the walls. Neither the contours, nor the colours, nor the general " atmosphere " of this bend of the Thames can have changed much in the last hundred and fifty years. The scene does not inspire awe, or ravish with an unearthly beauty ; the houses are mellow, but not venerable ; on a sunny afternoon the *genius loci* seems to say : " The French Revolution passed, tumults and wars and rhapsodies passed ; but this is civilisation, this is competence, this is establishment and a just harmony of the things most pleasant and most comfortable." At the end of the walk, behind the great old elm-tree whose wrinkled trunk is fixed in the stone pavement, there is a stone church with a squat tower and a little spire above it ; homely also, but English of an earlier day. On the north side of the quiet graveyard is a narrow and secluded walk, and amongst the monuments to be seen from this is a solid lichened structure surrounded by iron railings. It was erected, soon after the eighteenth century had closed, to the memory of Philip James Loutherbourgh, the painter, and the inscription states that—

With Talents brilliant and supereminent as an Artist
He united the still more envied Endowments of
a cultivated, enlarged and elegant Mind,
adding to both the supreme Qualities of the Heart,

which entitled him as a Man and a Christian to the
cordial Respect of the Wise and Good.
In him Science was associated with Faith, Piety with
Liberality,
Virtue with Suavity of Manners,
and the rational use of this World with the ennobling
hope of a world to come.
A deathless Fame will record his professional
Excellence,
but to the Hand of Friendship belongs the Office
of strewing on his Tomb those moral flowers
which displayed themselves in his Life
and which rendered him estimable as a Social Being.

Loutherbourgh's professional excellence is not now
so generally esteemed as it might be ; though he still
enjoys a modest honour at Greenwich Hospital and
at Dulwich. The epitaph—for even the longest
epitaph cannot be a full biography—makes no mention of some of his odder achievements, his friendship with Cagliostro, his invention of the Eidophu-
sicon, and his discovery, occluded by the breaking of
a crucible at the last moment, of the philosopher's
stone. Yet underneath its formal phraseology can
be perceived more sincerity than is general in " lapi-
dary inscriptions," and, whether or not it is complete
as the description of a particular man, it certainly
holds good as the formulation of the ideals of an age.
Mr. Chesterton has spoken of " The Victorian
Compromise " ; the Victorian Compromise was
far less perfect and positive than the Georgian Compromise. Compared with that it was little more than
a conspiracy of silence, among conspirators who

were mostly traitors. The Georgians, who were neither self-blinded nor fanatical, had made up their minds what they believed and what they wanted, what was " rational enjoyment " and what the qualities that made man " estimable as a Social Being." Their view of life appears to us limited ; but they held it, and they held it not without reason. Their poetry reflected their general outlook ; and processes analogous to those which led to their theory and practice in Art may be discovered in the other spheres of their activity.

In other words, there were reasons. All chapters may look alike in a history-book, and all noises may be equally subdued by virtue of their remoteness. But fever and convalescence, breakdown and recovery, abuse and protest, were things experienced even by persons who wore picturesque clothes, very queer, different from our own. Reconstruction, by the same token, was an idea familiar to the early eighteenth century, though perhaps the " blessed word " had not been invented. The seventeenth century had been, and not merely in England, a century of civil wars. The flowers of the Renaissance and the Reformation had brought forth their vivid and variegated fruit. The problem that faced men in all departments was that of the restoration of order. A *modus vivendi* had to be found, lest chaos should return. The lucidity and rationality of Dryden was a necessary corrective when Elizabethan luxuriance had run to seed in extravagant tropes, and when, largely under Donne's influence, ruggedness and obscurity had been cultivated to a point at which they threatened the complete ruin of poetry. Dryden

knew what he was doing ; Pope, when he talked of
" correctness," was not speaking of the artificial rules
of " one Boileau," but of the immortal laws of common sense. He wanted no obscurity, no wild hap-
hazard shots, no inaccuracies of phrase, no tangle of
irrelevant images, no harsh and discordant lines. His
garden may have been too tidy ; but his campaign
was waged against weeds, not against forest trees or
wild flowers. It was a necessary campaign, and the
victory overwhelmed the conquered and seriously
embarrassed the conquerors.

The eighteenth-century reconstruction was a
complete success. There probably never was a time
when taste was more uniform and when men were
more generally agreed about institutions. Under the
crust there were the Wesleyans, and the prisons
which John Howard threw open to the daylight, and
the weavers, who so puzzled Horace Walpole, and
the discontented peasantry—allowances must be
made for the pictures of a doctrinaire Radical—of
Caleb Williams. But these things caused no great
disturbance. They were not completely ignored.
Howard's campaign led to reforms ; it was Dr.
Johnson, a whole-hearted advocate of " subordina-
tion," who said that the test of every Government
was the provision it made for the poor ; Wilberforce
was a typical product of the century, which, for all
its scepticism about Utopias, was genuinely philan-
thropic. Nevertheless, the extreme politics of the
seventeenth and the nineteenth centuries scarcely
existed ; and the unity which marked the political
world was characteristic also of the artistic. Pope,
like Walpole, had his enemies ; but the opinions of

both were generally accepted. Pope was abused in Popean couplets, and Walpole was inveighed against on sound Whig principles. We were a nation of Whigs, and there were few recalcitrants. Blake was a late and a lonely figure, and Kit Smart (the century ended before the *Song to David* was recognised) was a conformist until he lost his senses. Even when men were aberrant in one way they retained a certain measure of respectability by an observance of convention in other ways. Incorrect morals did not seem so alarming when embodied in correct verse, and impropriety of sentiment was partially redeemed by propriety of diction. Extravagant opinions expressed in extravagant forms were almost unknown. There was no doubt at all that the seventeenth century was over. The Riot Act had been read and the disorderly mob had entirely dispersed.

Reaction, indisputably, went too far. Reaction usually does. Men living in the middle of things to which they object may be pardoned for a lack of perspective ; at any rate, they always exhibit it. A debauch of fantasy and freedom was followed by an orgy of order and common sense. The freedom had run to licence, the conventionalism ran to stiffness and pedantry. The rhapsodies of the "metaphysicals" were followed by poems from which the mystical element was almost entirely absent. Poets who had strained themselves to find new epithets and devise new images were followed oy poets who were overprone to use a constitutional stock of images and whose vocabulary was altogether too restricted and hackneyed. The contrast was like the contrast of Palladian and of Gothic architecture. Mr. Courthope,

who went as far as any man could in defence
of the eighteenth century, made a suggestion that
was ingenious but not adequate. He detected two
main elements in our poetic literature, the Poetry
of Romance and the Poetry of Manners, and argued
that, a wave of the former being exhausted, the
eighteenth century returned to the latter. It took
up, he said, the tradition of Chaucer and Shakespeare. But Shakespeare was all things, and if Chaucer
be merely a poet of manners, the eighteenth century
did not produce a man who could hold a candle to
him ; that breadth and freshness and gusto did not
come again. The eighteenth century may have had
the " wine," but it had little of the " Provencal
song." Its defects were defects of stiffness, of over-
restraint ; the term " enthusiast " it employed only
in reproach ; the music of its verse, though often
charming, was not varied ; the exultations of its
spirit were tempered ; it tended (though here and
there were exceptions all the more welcome because
of their rarity) to avoid expressing in their full force
its emotions concerning the things which move men
most. Its love songs are seldom passionate ; its landscapes have usually been supervised by the landscape gardener ; it made few contributions to the
body of our most ardent religious poetry ; and Dr.
Johnson was very representative of it in confessing
privately that the fear of death was a thing which
haunted him daily, whilst refraining from expressing
that fear in his verse. Juvenal, Martial and Horace
would have been at home in the century ; Virgil
would have found links with it ; the great Greeks
would have been alien to it. Much of its best verse

was written by clergymen of the Church of England, Erastians all, and by noble lords who read the Latin poets.

Yet there is as much sincerity in eighteenth-century verse as in that of other periods, whatever its restraints and taboos ; the transports were moderated, but the feeling was there ; and the general standard of technical accomplishment was high. Pope, Churchill and Hogarth, Gray, Goldsmith and Richard Wilson may have had their limitations, but the art of a century whose observation and whose sentiment were manifested in such men as those was not contemptible. The prose of the age, in comparison with the work of other ages, was relatively greater than its poetry ; its poetry may be admitted to be the poetry of a prose age. Accept this : read Langhorne and Akenside in the light not of Shelley nor of Browning, but of Burke, Johnson and the author of *Amelia*, and, when you have become accustomed to the quiet, the dignity, the formal phraseology, you will find in them manliness and tenderness, conviction and affection.

I think that to some extent appreciation of the eighteenth-century poets may revive in the near future ; such a revival would be, I believe, a useful and a significant thing. The eighteenth century is not the only century which ran to an extreme. Ever since the age of Shakespeare, who was a microcosm of the whole universe of poetry, the tendency has always been for the pendulum to swing too far one way or the other, towards what Mr. Courthorpe roughly and comprehensively called the Poetry of Romance or towards what he called the Poetry of

Manners. If the dangers of one generation have been complacency, formalism, lack of passion, those of another have been remoteness from common life, rhetorical verbiage, and a simulated excess of sensibility. Few, I suppose, would wish that all the characteristics of eighteenth-century poetry should again become dominant. The prevalent state of spirit and doctrine led some men, who might in another age have written poetry of the kind which we believe to be the highest, to devote themselves principally to what, with all its merits, was sublimated journalism. Pope himself, the greatest poetical wit, satirist and essayist we have, had it in him to be more than that ; many of his successors devoted themselves too much for our taste to controversy and satire, to the neat record of merely interesting urban observation. Satire and instruction may be the one delightful, and the other edifying ; but the sedulous cultivation of either in poetry is apt to cramp the heart and the imagination. " Sympathy : a Poem," and " An Essay on Immorality ; in Three Parts " do not need to be repeated. All the dexterity and charm of the Augustans and Georgians cannot prevent most of us from wishing that they had cultivated another mood and allowed their nobler emotions freer play. He who goes to poetry for exaltation, for pain, or for consolation will certainly not go to the eighteenth century as often as to others. Yet whatever they did— and, far more frequently than most people allow, they did write movingly as well as beautifully—the best of them can give us salutary lessons in exactitude and straightforwardness, honesty and the avoidance of over-statement. The bad poets have faults as gross as those of other ages ; the better poets, considered as artistic influences, would certainly not be so dangerous, by virtue of their mere mannerisms, as their predecessors the " metaphysicals." We may never achieve the union of the best qualities of all ages, in thought and expression ; but we may at least aim at it, so far as our conscious activity can go. The history of civilisation is the history of exaggerated reactions against doctrines, persons, institutions and tastes. It may be well on occasion to go to extremes : it is a mistake to be carried to them.

This book, however, is not intended to be an argument in a controversy, much less the manifesto of a Back-to-Queen-Anne movement. Mr. Williams likes the sort of thing that the eighteenth century did well, and he confesses to an especial fondness for small authors who have received less than their due. Opinions about the value of eighteenth-century poetry as compared with that produced in other ages may vary, and it is difficult to believe that there will ever come a time when many readers will regard it as one of the chief glories of our literature. But it is altogether beyond dispute that for a hundred years it has been neglected more than any other considerable body of English literature, and that many delightful eighteenth-century poems are only not appreciated because they are never read. Reaction, natural reaction, went so far that only a few of the most eminent eighteenth-century poets have been able to command a reluctant attention. Men have been scouring the libraries of the world for the feeblest of Elizabethan sonnet-sequences, and a hundred editors have been reprinting the Clevelands

and Cartwrights and Godolphins and Chamber-
laynes of the Caroline era, and pointing with ecstasy
at what Pope called the—

One simile that solitary shines
In the dry desert of a thousand lines.

It does no harm, and whenever a good thing is
rescued from oblivion we are so much the better off.
But the fact that the seventeenth century produced
greater poets than the eighteenth does not imply
that any seventeenth-century writer is better worth
consideration than any eighteenth-century writer.
Mr. Williams, in his collection, presents many
charming verses by minor poets, some of whom have
probably never been quoted since the death of Pitt.
There are very many more whom his readers will
encounter should he continue, as I hope he will, his
personally-conducted tours around the By-ways.
Let us assume, though it is a large assumption, that
the best things of Pomfret and Parnell, Dyer and
Akenside stand no longer in need of proclamation ;
that Blair and the Scotch poetesses and Mrs. Barbauld are at least partially known to everybody who
reads histories of English literature ; that there was
no need for Mr. Williams to subjoin Tickell's once
celebrated ballad to the two that he now reprints.
There are still dozens of poets who deserve a modest
rehabilitation, some even who did not even bask in
a contemporary sunshine as a compensation for the
absence of that posthumous fame to which poets so
invariably and so inexplicably aspire. Mr. Mason,
whose satirical poems, particularly " The Dean and

the Squire " and the delicious " Epistle to Milles " (if he wrote it), are excellent, cut a sufficient figure ; his verse pamphlets are perhaps commoner than any in the bound collections of the time. Mickle and Sir William Jones, Whitehead, Savage and Robert Ferguson, in all of whom something worth having is to be found, were all widely read during, or just after, their own time. So, in whole or in part, were John Byrom, Lord Nugent, Sir Charles Hanbury Williams, Logan and Bruce. There are obscurer men still who do not deserve to be ignored. In anthologies of a hundred years ago may be found considerable selections from Scott of Amwell, Lovibond and Penrose, of which parts have withered like plants cut off at the roots, but parts are still fresh to the sympathetic reader. I have never in any modern book seen an allusion to the " Monody " (on his dead wife) of Cuthbert Shaw, a reckless and unfortunate man whose genius was acknowledged by Dr. Johnson, who dealt sparingly in his commendations of contemporary poets. The " Monody " was a famous piece in its day and for long afterwards. Shaw's picture of his wife's death in childbirth and his reflections on the infant she has left him (" My little darling !— dearer to me grown By all the tears thou'st caused —O strange to hear ! Bought with a life yet dearer than thy own ") are profoundly moving ; and how well he employed the idiom of his time to express natural feeling may be illustrated by the image he uses to show the probable course of his own struggles against a cruelty that cannot be undone :

Thus the poor bird, by some disastrous fate,
　　Caught and imprison'd in a lonely cage,
Torn from its native fields, and dearer mate,
　　Flutters awhile, and spends its little rage :
But, finding all its efforts weak and vain,
　　No more it pants and rages for the plain ;
Moping a while, in sullen mood
　　Droops the sweet mourner—but, ere long,
Prunes its light wings and pecks its food,
　　And meditates the song :
Serenely sorrowing, breathes its piteous case,
　　And with its plaintive warblings saddens all
　　　　the place.

Far worse poems are now on everybody's lips ; but
even the modern enthusiasts for the eighteenth
century have overlooked it. They have overlooked
with more excuse Charles Jenner's "Town Eclogues,"
charming excursions in the manner of Gay which
were never well known at any time. There are good
things in James Scott's "Odes," and many scattered
passages of merit in the satires of Combe and others.
It is not my business to tell Mr. Williams, who knows
all about it, where to pursue his researches ; I have
merely mentioned a few names which do not occur
in his book as an illustration of my belief that there
are far more good fish in Mr. Williams's sea (or
ornamental water, if you like) than have yet come
out of it.

TENNYSON*

ALL the oracles of the Victorian age have been passing under a cloud. Those " prophets," like Browning and Morris, who were but moderately applauded in their own day are now rather neglected than abused ; but many of their more popular contemporaries are frequently spoken of by this generation as though they were mere tiresome humbugs. Carlyle is a dyspeptic who ranted in very bad English ; Dickens is a maudlin sentimentalist and absurd caricaturist whose English was equally bad ; Ruskin is an emasculate prig who mingled pious exhortations with laborious purple patches ; and Tennyson a poet born to be bound in morocco for the use of girls' schools, the coeval and similitude of the antimacassar, the oleograph, the Albert Memorial, and the Crystal Palace—whose " long laborious miles," it is true, he celebrated. Against great popularity there is bound to be some reaction, and there is usually some element of truth, however slight, in the bitter attacks made upon great men who have been treated as superhuman. " They use me as a lesson-book at schools," grumbled Tennyson, " and they will call me ' that horrible Tennyson.' " Even Aristides, the young in time feel, cannot have been quite so just as all that, however lofty his forehead and grave his deportment : in any

* " The Works of Tennyson." With the author's notes. Edited by Hallam, Lord Tennyson. Macmillan, Eversley Edition, 9 vols. (And many other editions.)
" The Suppressed Poems of Tennyson." Edited by J. C. Thomson.
" The Life of Lord Tennyson, by his Son." Macmillan.

event they are sick of hearing his name. It is the common lot of the famous in their own day ; their immediate successors tend to concentrate on the obverse of the medal : when all that can be said against them has been said they reach the position they deserve. The tide has already set strongly in Dickens's favour (the general public never deserted him), and it probably will not be long before critics tire of ignoring the better part of Tennyson's poetry. But with him, as with most of the Victorians, there is more in it than a mere automatic revulsion against idolatry. In no age—not even in our own—did poets and essayists more strenuously involve themselves in the discussions of the day than they did in the middle of the nineteenth century. In almost all writers of all ages there is a certain topical—we may even say journalistic—element, partly open, partly vaguely diffused as a tinge or tone, which appeals to one generation as it never will to another. In many of the Victorians, absorbed in concern for the future of religion and the State, this element is very large. Their posterity finds it dull, stale, platitudinous ; never more so than in Tennyson, who preached " the golden mean." We have our own controversialists who are more closely in touch with the latest aspects of our problems and the momentary complexion of our minds. Hence an added impetus to a reaction which the reputations of all writers popular in their own day suffer in some degree. The more, by virtue of a man's " topicality," his preoccupation with the changing surface of things and his infection by mere fashion in opinion he " dates," the more violent is the reaction against him.

Victorian writers themselves, confident and complacent and shortsighted as they are often represented to be, were no blinder to this than we are. Matthew Arnold, in his essay on Joubert, puts it very clearly ; he was quite probably aware that many even of his his own works would mean less to later generations than they did to his own day :

> The acceptableness of Shakespeare's criticism depends upon its inherent truth ; the acceptableness of Scribe's upon its suiting itself, by its subject-matter, ideas, mode of treatment, to the taste of the generation that hears it. But the taste and ideas of one generation are not those of the next. This next generation in its turn arrives ; first its sharpshooters, its quick-witted, audacious light troops ; then the elephantine main body. The imposing array of its predecessor it confidently assails, riddles it with bullets, passes over its body. It goes hard then with many once popular reputations, with many authorities once oracular.

He gives Macaulay, then recently dead, as a probable example of those writers who sink into oblivion. He may have been wrong there, but he was certainly right in saying that authors, great and less, only survive by virtue of their criticism (to use his awkward word, which requires qualifying or explaining in this connection)of those elements in human life which do not materially change. Arnold's tracts on the English educational system may have been valuable, perhaps indispensable ; but even had they been written in admirable verse the day would certainly have come when they would have been very little read, and then only as amusing pamphlets in a dead controversy, or by virtue of their having been composed by the author of " The Scholar-Gipsy." This does not necessarily prove that he was wrong in writing them. The poet is not the only man who is essential to society, poetry is not the only work by which a man can justify his existence, and it is arguable that even a great poet might properly immolate his art in the interests of doctrine in an age when what he conceived as civilisation was in danger. Both Arnold and Tennyson throughout their lives believed that England and Europe were threatened with collapse. Tennyson was, on principle, more optimistic about it, but the social peril presented itself so forcibly as to fortify what was no doubt a strong natural inclination in him to regard as a ministry any course of life he might pursue.

For it is obvious that Tennyson deliberately dedicated himself as a poet to what he conceived to be the service of humanity. It would be clear enough if we had nothing but his works to go on ; every sort of lesson is inculcated in terms, and there is a pervading set intention to present the elevating and to avoid the deliberately noxious. His political verses are a sort of companions to the works of Walter Bagehot. He was a principal agent in that process of " reconciling religion and science " which the contemporaries of Darwin deemed to be necessary, bridging the gulf between Bishop Wilberforce and Bradlaugh. With every volume he gave his readers draughts of medicine labelled " Law and Order," " Constitutionalism," " Evolutionary Reform,"

" The Limits of Feminism," " International Amity,"
" Enlightened Imperialism," " Enlightened Paci-
fism," " Enlightened Self-defence," " The Necessity of Theism." No poet has made it more clear
that he was delivering a message to his age and what
the message was. One sometimes has the feeling
that, though Bacon could not have written Shakespeare, he might have written a good many passages
in Tennyson. But those who care for it may find
more evidence than this of the nature of his ambition.
" My father would say," writes his son, " ' One must
distinguish from among the poets the great sage
poets of all, who are both great thinkers and great
artists, like Æschylus, Dante, and Goethe.' " He
always meant, if possible, to be one of those. He
said in terms that a poet's comments on public affairs
should be " statesmanlike " ; he conceived of himself as what Arthur Hallam would have been :

> A potent voice in Parliament,
> A steadfast pillar in the storm,

who should be occupied with :

> Turning to scorn with lips divine
> The falsehood of extremes.

" Molière," he said, " is the greatest French poet :
he is so sane." The judgment may be disputed ; but
the reason given is significant. At the call of conscience Tennyson cultivated sanity and set himself
to promulgate what he believed to be the counsels
of sanity. He was during the greater part of his writing hours dominated by his sense of responsibility.

He dedicated himself : he was to interpret and to guide, to console and to uplift his own age. It may well be argued—the question will not be discussed here—that his success in that enterprise was such as to have justified his decision : that he was of immense value. It is impossible precisely to assess the influence of those great Victorian writers who, in an age of transition, spent their lives fighting materialism, or undisciplined and ignorant idealism, or both : but it is certain that none was more widely influential than Tennyson. It is difficult to put one's finger on particular places and say that here and here are the social fruits of his thought. But it was not for nothing that throughout a generation he was quoted in every pulpit, in every scientific work, and by every political party, which found in him the expression of those elements of truth and justice which it was most certain that it possessed. And he was no mere sounding-board, no harp vibrating to every wind that blew. He did think, his thought was as independent as any man's, and, familiar though much of it has grown, we have only to read the acknowledgments paid to it by contemporaries of undisputed eminence and originality in every sphere of work to realise that he actually took a considerable share in influencing public opinion, and that if we hold that his particular views were salutary in that age, his influence was one to which our civilisation must owe a great debt. The mere " spell-binding " effect of his great treasury of phrases which became familiar to millions must have been immense : but, beyond all that, those who themselves thought took him seriously as a thinker. He made scientists pause and politicians reflect : he was in his poetry a link between every sort of professional world, a sort of club, or even church, in which the soldier met the don, and the street-corner revolutionist the Cabinet Minister. Even Herbert Spencer, whom we cannot imagine perusing any poet of our own day, read him, found interest in him, and sent him " The Principles of Psychology " as a sort of expansion of a stanza in " The Two Voices." If the records of controversial literature be a test, he coloured the speculation—which presumably means moulding the actions—of his day as no other thinker in England has ever done. His principal tenets may be accessible in the works of other writers, but he remains just as important as a channel. In short, even if—as it will be presently contended—he became a " sage " rather *contra naturam*, he certainly did the purely contemporary part of a sage's work.

But the permanence of his achievement, the poetic quality of his work was certainly adversely affected by his conception of his function. To the first and most obvious point attention has already been drawn. He argued ; he made " pronouncements " on matters of topical interest. Froude said he had " this relative superiority even to Shakespeare, that he speaks the thoughts and speaks to the perplexities and misgivings of his own age " : but superiority of that kind could only exist in the eyes of his own age. Much of his genuine work has a tinge of the ephemeral interest ; and the consciousness of a mission led him to write a good deal that was not poetry and was not born in the conditions that make for poetry. He was angry when people thought he

had written the " Ode on the Duke of Wellington "
to order merely because he was Poet Laureate ; he
certainly wrote a good deal that never came from a
poetic state of mind and heart. The best-known
illustrations are the best to recall. Phrases like " one
flag, one fleet, one throne," and

> Freedom broadening slowly down
> From precedent to precedent

are admirably terse statements of fact, or supposed
fact ; they became current coin because they summarised current opinions ; and being in verse they
had that kind of mnemonic value which attaches to
all sorts of other metrical statements, such as
" Thirty days hath September." The rational
Tennyson held that theory about freedom ; but this
phrase does not suggest that it exalted him. Phrases
more imaginative can be found by the score in
Bagehot and in Burke ; the image is the sort of thing
which Mr. Winston Churchill, in his graver moments, can equal and often better. Hundreds of
Tennyson's lines are simple statements of the sort,
often turned with consummate elegance, but made
in cold blood ; lines which he could have written
at any hour of any day as a man writes a leading
article. Nobody, it may be admitted, ever concocted
verses more dexterously ; but concoction is concoction. The civic sense may lead a man to burn a
good poem ; if that alone leads him to write a poem,
he cannot expect it to be a good one.

And no doubt the practice of manufacturing verse
for conscience' sake encouraged the habit of manufacturing verse which had no surface relations with

controversy. Only such a habit could explain the dull dead series of his worst poems, works only redeemed by beautiful natural similes drawn from his notebook and pinned, like butterflies, to artificial surroundings. He faked ; he is not all of a piece ; much of his writing did not really come out of himself. That is where he differed from poets of a less sophisticated kind. If you really like Wordsworth, knowing what is good Wordsworth, you will still have an affection for bad Wordsworth ; but nobody who knows the difference between good and bad likes bad Tennyson. And there is a great deal of it. There might be less : it is unfortunate that the authorised editions always open with the false and feeble juvenilia written before he could reasonably be expected to know whence poetry comes. But we can find wildernesses of tedious verse in him without resorting to puerilities of the type of

> Smiling, frowning, evermore
> Thou art perfect in love-lore,
> Ever varying Madeleine.

Many of his short poems are empty prettinesses ; there are unreadable acres in " The Princess " ; his shorter tales are mostly novelettes with but a semblance of life. They give the impression that they proceeded merely from the reflection, " It is now time to compose another narrative," but there are other weaknesses in them than those which spring from lack of inspiration. There is not only no life in narratives like " Dora," " Audley Court," " Walking to the Mail," " The Lake " : not only are the patches of beautiful embedded description surrounded

by dull tracts of skilfully versified prose, but the
stories and characters embody thoughts and ideals
which we find trivial and foolish. If it be difficult
to understand how the artist of " The Lotos-Eaters "
could become the artist of " The May-Queen," it
is also difficult to understand how the brain which
conceived " Lucretius " and " The Vision of Sin "
could be satisfied with the superficial saccharinities
which are held up for admiration in those stories.
It is those tales that have led the hasty to form an
impression of Tennyson as a sentimental confec-
tioner of prettiness who loved the mawkish, and
who particularly liked simpering and blushing girls.
There certainly does seem to have been an odd strain
in his attitude towards women. His pictures of them
are frequently suited to be pendants to the pictures
of Mr. Marcus Stone. These maidens are to be found
among the roses ; their eyes are " a bashful azure" ;
their fond lovers will indicate their Arcadian tastes
in phrases like :

> While dreaming on your damask cheek,
> The dewy sister-eyelids lay.

There must have been in Tennyson some inclination
towards that kind of clinging, blushing, speechless
maiden in muslin, the notion of whom has been found
repellent by a generation which asks that women
should have, at least, something of Rosalind's, if not
something of Penthesilea's, spirit. He was, as a story-
teller, preoccupied with the mere surface of court-
ship, and could fittingly close with " There comes a
sound of marriage bells " ; and he resembled other
writers of sentimental novelettes in this, that he

continually recurred, for a plot—though without ever properly exploring the situation—to the love of a person of higher social status towards one of lower. The subject of " The Lord of Burleigh " was almost an obsession with him : when it wasn't a " village maiden " it was a miller's daughter or a gardener's daughter or a nurse's daughter. Whatever may have driven him to these stories, so commonplace and superficial in treatment, it may at least be supposed that his usual avoidance of any deeper treatment of the relations between people, and of the passion of man for woman in particular, was due to that habit of restraint which his sage's conscience engendered. When we come to a poem like " Lucretius " or " The Vision of Sin " we wonder what has been happening : we do not want all poetry to be as grim as this, but, at least, we have a feeling that the poet is letting himself go and telling the truth. Usually we have the sense that he is not telling the truth and is afraid to let himself go. Every word must be weighed ; no word must be spoken which could do harm ; temperance was what the people most needed, and temperate the poet must be ; it was very seldom that he let us see his own more violent emotions, and he smoothed such things over when writing of other people ; the sense of obligation probably led him also to think that he must write stories that the whole population would understand and like. The result is a hothouse feeling ; a sensation of stuffiness ; a need of wind, sun, and rain. And the practice of grave responsibility has contributed towards the picture, partly false, of him which many of the present generation have formed. He set up a plaster cast of himself, and they see him as a plaster-cast Bard, noble of brow, wide of eye, firm of mouth, full-bearded. He was not unassisted in the operation. Even in early days it is evident that he had very little criticism and a good deal of adulation from his friends. " Vex not thou the poet's mind, With thy shallow wit . . . Thou canst not fathom it " was a juvenile straw which showed which way the wind might be expected to blow. He was already on the way to a pompous altitude and a pontifical position. The Cambridge set were determined to send him forth on his mission, and spoke of him everywhere as a portent. His intimate friends in later life were not artists, and conspired to put him on a pedestal. He was " the Bard " to them, and they would have left him uncriticised, even if he had not, as he had, grown hyper-sensitive to criticism. That very sensitiveness, possibly, was accentuated by the difficulty of his self-imposed task of philosopher and guide : at any rate, it was there. Very likely he often forgot to criticise, or to remember, himself : certainly his sense of humour was often out of employment. But never did Tennyson become as serene as Goethe was and as Sophocles—to whom as a social influence Jebb compared him—may be supposed to have been. The weight of Empire might rest on him ; he might correspond with Mr. Gladstone about the need of coupling a Redistribution Bill with the Franchise Bill ; he might regret that he had not had a peerage when young enough to speak in the House of Lords ; he might consort with all the gravest seniors in all the Services and professions ; he might, restrained by conviction, write a great deal of verse which could have been the work of a curate in whose mouth butter wouldn't melt. But there was something in him beyond the Laureate burdened with the cares of office, the responsible Bard who put things into verse that were proper to prose, and refused to publish one line of prose because he thought it might impair the sacred mystery of his Bardship. There were elements in his personality and in his tastes to which he did not allow free play, and which would have produced a larger volume of great poetry had he allowed them free play.

Tennyson's Life by his son is a work of great value and interest, the fruit of immense industry and devotion. But there is a great deal left out of it. The poet himself was always vehement against the disclosure of dead writers' private lives : he complained (in his son's words) that " the world likes to know about the roughnesses, eccentricities, and defects of a man of genius, rather than what he really is." There is truth in this ; yet if too much is concealed we can never know what a man is. We know that the serene, stately, almost priestly personage who paces across the pages of the Life is not, in externals, like the Tennyson whom the old among us still remember : that black, swarthy, unkempt old gipsy, with fierce eyes, who could be so gruff and so caustic and so silent. He was not always what he was at eighty : the beautiful young Tennyson of Lawrence's too-little known portrait probably had other ways, equally unfamiliar to us. At all events, the portrait in the " Life " is a conventional Academy portrait, a representation at once more and less than human.

The private stories one hears about him are as much in character with each other as are those about the Duke of Wellington ; they are by no means in character with the conventional image of the Laureate. Possibly the story about stays and braces is not true ; but the ejaculations were in exactly the same grumpy direct vein as that which he growled out to the young caller who asked how he was : " Old and ugly, old and ugly ! " A thoroughly representative picture of the Tennyson of oral tradition is given in Addington Symonds's memoranda. Symonds in 1865 was allowed to join his elders after dinner : Woolner, Gladstone, Tennyson and Holman Hunt. The conversation was a duologue between Gladstone and Tennyson. They talked of the Jamaica revolt : the statesman was eloquent, oratorical, sentimental. The poet " did not argue " ; he merely kept on grumbling " niggers are tigers, niggers are tigers." He described his own temperament : " If the fiery gulf of Curtius opened in the City, I would leap at once into it on horseback. But if I had to reflect on it, no . . . I could not wait six hours in a square expecting a battery's fire."

Tennyson all the while kept drinking glasses of port and glowering round the room through his spectacles. His moustache hides the play of his mouth, but as far as I could see, that feature is as grim as the rest. He has cheek-bones carved out of iron.

A " broad, coarse, grotesque " man, says Symonds, " with huge, unwieldy hands, fit for moulding clay or dough ; he became gentle and profoundly earnest

when talking of God and the soul." And if we are
not shown the Tennyson who talked to people, still
less are we shown the Tennyson who communed
with himself. He was one of the most reserved of
men : it is likely that few materials exist on which a
history of his true inner mind, *la vraie verité*, could
be based. Was he or was he not conscious throughout
life of an internal struggle between two Tennysons ?
There is an early letter of Arthur Hallam's to him
which contains this significant passage :

> You say pathetically, " Alas for me ! I have
> more of the Beautiful than the Good." Remember
> to your comfort that God has given you to see the
> difference. Many a poet has gone on blindly in his
> artist pride.

We see him here putting duty and liking in opposi-
tion, fearful of following beauty, in distress about
the course he should pursue. It is likely that the
fight there indicated went on throughout life : the
conflict between temperament and conscience, between natural genius and conviction, between the
responsible Bard and the born romantic. He cannot
but have been permanently aware of that self which
said that " Keats, had he lived, would have been
the greatest of us," and confessed to having been
haunted all his life with the words, " far, far away,"
as well as the self which deliberately laboured to be
" a great sage poet." The teachers—though Shakespeare, except in so far as all tender, generous, and
tolerant men must be, was not one of them—may
be the greatest of poets. It may have been inevitable
that Tennyson, in the era of the Reform Bill, should

have been forced to think of his social duty first and foremost. The fact remains that his genius was not of the austere kind ; that the unique part of him was not made to expound a gospel (whether sane or insane) like Shelley, nor to discuss women's emancipation like John Stuart Mill, nor to tell village tales like Jane Austen. It is not for us to despise their moral rectitude, but it is certain that neither he nor Arnold—he even less than Arnold—were born to be prophets. I do not suggest for a moment that any theme in the world may not be the subject of great poetry : but poetry, to be true poetry, and of permanent interest, must grow out of a man naturally. Moral and political themes have moved other poets : they sometimes inspired Tennyson himself. But unless a man's work springs from emotion, from things powerfully felt, it is as poetry worthless : and the things which moved the Poet Tennyson most powerfully and surely were not usually the things with which the Sage Tennyson was most concerned, and the Sage Tennyson frequently prevented the Poet Tennyson from feeling and writing as he was naturally inclined to do. It is a matter of common observation that the early volumes of 1842 contain a far larger proportion of Tennyson's finest work than do the voluminous pages which followed them, and that many of those of his poems which most clearly " live " were written in his twenties. Almost all his best work, whether early or late, is the work which is least like a " sage's." We can only write beautifully when the heart is welling with spontaneous love. It is not by the moral framework but by its landscapes that " The Palace of Art " lives : the things which preserve it are those very things which Tennyson's " soul " is telling him, in the poem, to turn his back on. If the sensuous enjoyment of beauty be the devil, it was to the devil that Tennyson sang his best tunes. " St. Agnes Eve," " The Lotos-Eaters," " The Morte d'Arthur," the songs in " The Princess " : with none of these has the sage the remotest connection : in fact he may have disapproved of them as tending to stimulate the cultivation of an enervating melancholy. Tennyson at his poetic best is not a rugged prophet, but the most languorous and lamenting of the romantics. Arnold found the crown and essence of romanticism in the lines :

> Some lady of the lake
> Lone-sitting by the shores of old romance.

The lines, though Wordsworth's, might have been Tennyson's : it is curious that when he is at his best that very picture, the picture of a lonely, usually deserted, lady in beautiful surroundings is recurrent with him. There are the two Marianas : there is " Œnone " : there is " The Lady of Shalott." " The Dream of Fair Women " is a collection of them, and the forlorn Guinevere at the end of the " Idylls " may properly be grouped with them. Even as a good poet Tennyson was more versatile than any English poet since Shakespeare. The author of " The Lotos-Eaters " wrote " The Revenge," " The Talking Oak," " The Northern Farmer," and " Will Waterproof's Monologue." But in the majority of his good poems he is very closely akin to Keats on the one hand and the Pre-Raphaelites on the other. The spectacle of courage gave him unusually fiery vigour when he wrote " The Revenge " and a few other poems ; as a rule if he wishes to convey an impression of strength in action he tries to do it by crowding his incorrigibly quiet rhythms with an abnormal number of consonants in the manner of " clang battleaxe and clash brand." He was fundamentally a poet of the other kind. In very little of his best work does the " Victorian outlook " which is so much disliked appear. The passages most admired in his political and philosophical poems are landscape settings or images drawn from nature ; of his songs the best, such as " Break, Break, Break " and " Tears, Idle Tears," are spontaneous cries produced by a sorrow which is as universal as it is unreasoning.

Grief here moved him, as it did often during the years which saw the product of his most genuine inspirations being poured into the mould of " In Memoriam " ; as it did when he wrote " In the Garden at Swainston " and " In the Valley of Cauteretz." Can we find even in Burns and Heine anything more direct than these ? " It came in a moment," he said of one of them ; of many of his poems he could not even have said that the nucleus of them, the first seminal lines, came in a moment. They were set-pieces originating in the reasoning faculty ; they were composed with prodigious skill ; many of them " interested " his contemporaries ; but his habit of composition, encouraged by this conception of his task, has resulted in the present appearance of his collected works, an appearance as of a basket of flowers shrivelled by the fumes and smirched by the soot of Victorian civilisation.

But he remains. This essay was begun with the object of calling attention to his merits, to the mass of his good poetry, which has recently been too much questioned and too much ignored. It has resolved itself largely into an attempt to diagnose some of his defects ; but it is perhaps as well frankly to admit them if one desires to say that the attempts to deny him a place among the great English poets are ridiculous. Not all even of his " philosophical " poetry was written ceremonially or is of ephemeral interest. " In Memoriam " not only communicates a strong and ageless human feeling, it is not only crowded with human landscapes, but it presents the problem of Time and Eternity in a manner in which it must present itself to many brooding spirits in all generations. That poem, in its essence, does not date at all. It is true that certain of its details would not have been present had the bones of the plesiosaurus never been discovered : but in essentials the objects of Tennyson's contemplation and the processes through which he goes are part of the permanent experience of the race. There is nothing outworn in it ; it is as fresh as ever it was ; its argument will constantly be repeated so long as men think of love and death and God ; it was repeated recently, in "The Undying Fire," by Mr. H. G. Wells, through all its stages up to the purely subjective and emotional conclusion. There is no nobler elegy, and no more genuine or better-shaped record of spiritual experience of the kind, in the language. He might, given his emotional faculties, have produced a greater number of lovely songs : he produced some, and the poems mentioned in the last paragraphs do not exhaust the catalogue of his complete and perfect works from " Mariana " to " Crossing the Bar " (which he wrote at eighty-one), whilst passages of pure poetry are scattered even in the most sterile places. His achievement as a poet was great, though it might have been greater ; his gifts of sight and speech, both those which work spontaneously and those which are consciously exercised, were extraordinary. Except when he was utterly uninspired by his theme he could not help writing exquisite music ; even when he was manufacturing he managed the artificial style—the style of the set funeral oration or the academic eulogy—more skilfully than any man before or since. He used with ease an enormous vocabulary, yet scarcely ever an obscure or a too recondite word ; and the minuteness of his observation is only equalled by the exactitude with which he chooses words to convey precisely what he sees. Many of his irreplaceable phrases about natural phenomena have become a part of our speech. Any detail in nature from a stormy sky to the black buds of the ash excited him, and was noted and recorded by him in words which could not be changed except with loss, though another poet might have seen with other eyes and made pictures of another kind. Occasionally the neatness with which he places every outline and colour is almost intolerable, especially when, as was his habit, he transferred into not wholly appropriate surroundings some picture from nature which had gone into his notebook by a Welsh waterfall, on an East Anglian shore, or " in the museum at Christiania." But the exactitude of his descriptions of detail is usually as satisfying to the artist as to the natural historian. He could describe anything. We may go beyond skies, trees, birds, and flowers, and find him describing a pasty :

> And half cut down, a pasty costly made,
> Where quail and pigeon, lark and leveret lay
> Like fossils of the rock, with golden yolks
> Imbedded and injellied.

If one is not hungry its realism makes one physically sick. He knew what he could do ; often he took pains to redeem a bad poem by "imbedding" good landscapes in it, frequently at the close where they left the reader happy. They are scattered everywhere ; he would make a note about a flower and use it as an image in a poem on the British Constitution ; it is incongruous, but it remains good in itself. Many of his descriptive phrases have the added power of suggesting more than they say, and he was as great a master of the set complete landscape as of the detail. There are few of the " Idylls " and few pages of " In Memoriam " where one does not find a complete scene seized and made perpetual. The whole English countryside, the whole English climate, are within his covers ; until Mr. Bridges he has had no rival in perception or in delineation. Tennyson's landscapes are the work of a man whose subtle sense told him, when he was writing " Mariana," to substitute " pear " for " peach " in the lines :

> The rusted nails fell from the knots
> That held the peach to the gable-wall.

Every feature is in its place, every epithet seems, and for a poet of this kind is, the one epithet. This gift was fully developed from the start. " The Gardener's Daughter" is a sickly and unconvincing poem. There is a good deal in it in the key of :

> Ah, one rose,
> One rose, but one, by those fair fingers cull'd,
> Were worth a hundred kisses press'd on lips
> Less exquisite than thine.

But it is there we find as clear a picture as he ever gave :

> A league of grass, wash'd by a slow broad stream,
> That, stirr'd with languid pulses of the oar,
> Waves all its lazy lilies, and creeps on,
> Barge-laden, to three arches of a bridge
> Crown'd with the minster towers.

He called Virgil a " lord of language " ; he was certainly one himself. Where he fails, where his words are dull (or as frequently happens, too pompously magniloquent) it is where he is writing without inspiration, where the balloon of language sags for want of inflation. Let a poet's language be considered, but the impulse behind it must be genuine. But whenever the impulse was strong he could do everything that could be done with words ; not only were they perfectly chosen for the making of distinctions, but he had mastered them for every sort of elegance of expression, and he never had an imaginative conception to which he was not equal. He was, as a rule, an elaborate and an ornamental writer. He was

unconsciously parodying himself when he said of
Edwin Morris " Poet-like he spoke " :

> My love for Nature is as old as I ;
> But thirty moons, one honeymoon to that,
> And three rich sennights more, my love for her.

When in " Amphion " he defended the poet, who
was a humble mountain-weed as against him who was
" half-conscious of the garden squirt," he certainly
was not defending himself. Unlike Keats's in the
Odes, his art did not altogether conceal itself. The
slightest chilliness and one is conscious of the
screwed-up eye and the search for the (somewhat
too plentiful) adjective. But his talent for ornament
was unsurpassed, and he had an Elizabethan gift
for that sort of trope which is so imaginative as hardly
to deserve the name :

> Sighs
> Which perfect Joy, perplex'd for utterance,
> Stole from her sister Sorrow.

One reads that sort of thing with a shock of delight,
and in Tennyson one finds it continually. All his
gifts, and all his faults, were exhibited in the ambitious work which was so eulogised in his day, and
has been so neglected in ours. The defects of the
" Idylls of the King " are many and obvious.
" Nature brings not back the Mastodon " ; an epic
is difficult ; and if Tennyson refused to write about
Job because he could not do better than his original
he might equally have shrunk from a comparison
with Malory. The moral compulsion was so strong

on him that he produced in King Arthur a hero
who, although he was confessed the "ideal man "
of Mr. Gladstone, gives the ordinary reader a chill.
We prefer Lancelot ; we are sure that Tennyson's
Guinevere would not have betrayed Tennyson's
Arthur had Arthur not been inhuman to her. Yet
even Arthur is often the mouthpiece for noble
speeches ; many of the subordinate characters are
remarkably vivid ; some of the subordinate stories
are deliciously told ; and the " best things are done
best." It is not only that these stories are strewn
with classic lines such as :

The wide-wing'd sunset of the misty marsh

and

Fall, as the crest of some slow-arching wave,
Heard in dead night along that table-shore,
Drops flat, and after the great waters break
Whitening for half a league, and thin themselves
Far over sands marbled with moon and cloud
From less and less to nothing ;

it is also that there are sustained passages where not
only is the eye delighted with pictures and the ear
with music, but the heart is held in suspense by the
doubtful issue of human struggle or the tragic close
of long and heroic action. " Lancelot and Elaine "
is not a mere tapestry ; the parting of Arthur and
Guinevere may move even those whom Arthur's
composure revolts ; and the most complimentary
thing one can say of the last idyll is that it is still vivid
and still eloquent when one has read for the tenth

time the incomparable chapter of Malory. Tennyson was not primarily a story-teller, and his narrative verse does tend at times to settle down into an even croon. But many of his detractors would do well if they could make their stories move as straightforwardly as the " Idylls " move, and better if they could contract something of the chivalrous spirit that informs the " Idylls." At times one seems to detect in the unmitigated abuse of them a kind of grudge against nobility.

The pure fountain of his poetry did not flow freely ; his aims were divided ; his personality is likely to command rather respect, mingled with slight irritation, than ardent affection. Poets will write poems about Shelley and Keats, but nobody will ever write a poem or play (at any rate, a good one) about Tennyson. Nevertheless—as would be clearly seen were an adequate selection (in which much from the " Idylls " would be included) to be made—he left a great deal of beautiful, and some superb, poetry which communicates the permanent pleasures of the race and expresses the deepest feelings of its heart, and which will stir and delight men in every age. And as a conscious craftsman his contemporaries were not far wrong in mentioning him in the same breath as Milton.

MATTHEW ARNOLD

M ATTHEW ARNOLD was born a hundred years ago, and died in 1888. I may briefly recapitulate what everybody knows. He was at Rugby under his father, Dr. Arnold, and at Rugby and Oxford with Clough, whose name was for long bracketed with his, whose fame is now completely overshadowed by that of Arnold. For most of his adult life he was an active, enlightened, and useful inspector of schools, and for ten years he coupled that occupation with the Professorship of Poetry at Oxford. Most of his poetry was written before he was fifty ; much of the best before he was thirty-five. His later years were given up almost entirely to controversy and a sustained propaganda on behalf of culture and morality, as he conceived them. His collected works, in fifteen volumes, were published in 1904-5 ; an official biography was forbidden by him.

There were fifteen volumes of the collected works. What part of them may be expected to " survive " ? It may be too early to say definitely that his polemic and expository work has gone, or will go. Probably a few readers will always be acquainted with "Friendship's Garland" and "Culture and Anarchy." A few find their way to the " Letters of Junius," and discover that, once begun, they are well worth reading ; it is difficult to conceive that there will ever come a time when nobody discovers how amusing " Friendship's Garland " is and how easy and elegant the prose in its companions. Yet these works

were journalism, though a very elevated kind of
journalism, and it is unlikely that they can ever recover a wide popularity. They were aimed at a particular generation, and they are full of topical references. In so far as they contain social truths, these
are truths which must always be restated in the light
of new conditions as the face of society changes. He
was an eloquent and valuable enemy of materialism
and advocate of a humane society ; the argument
must constantly be sustained, but much of his detail
no longer applies. In so far as his books deal with the
permanent universal problems of religion and morality, they have lost their audience. Honest as Arnold
was, hard as he strove to construct a gospel for himself and the world, his convictions were not passion-
ately held, and his sermons were not such as to give
refreshment to the spiritually thirsty. " Literature
and Dogma " and the rest of them, ably and beautifully written as they are, were only contributions
to a discussion. He, Dr. Arnold's son, a man in whom
an academic training was united with a haunting
sense of duty, was irresistibly drawn into those
debates which were only avoided by a few pre-
Raphaelites who withdrew behind the arras to escape
an ugly and blatant world. Many great men took
part in them, and many effective and ingenious dis-
putants, from Newman to Maurice, from Huxley
to Bradlaugh. They influenced their time, but their
essays and lectures and speeches have mostly faded.
Only great intellectual power, great beauty of form,
or vivid and passionate expression can find such
things readers after their immediate purpose has
been served ; and Arnold's prose works mostly do

not cross the frontiers of suave, earnest, dexterous journalism. He was ambitious enough. He did his utmost to supply his age with the religion which it lacked, a religion which might be accepted by all who felt the need. It was not accepted, and now that the ephemeral debating element in his pages has lost its savour, his fabric has hardly more than a historical interest.

Everybody knew Mr. Arnold's position then. It is not so exactly apprehended now. He did his conscientious best to retain as much of Christianity as was possible if his reason was to be satisfed. " Theology " was dismissed. Step by step he discarded the Trinity, miracles, the resurrection, " the phantasmagorical advent of Christ." He must remain agnostic about immortality and a personal God. There was left " morality touched with emotion," " a stream of tendency," " a power not ourselves making for righteousness," whose existence might be deduced from the fate of nations which had abandoned righteousness, and the happiness and direct testimony of those persons who had pursued it. His longing for belief was real ; his certainty that civilisation was in need of it was so strong that the spectacle of sectarian dispute over what he thought the subsidiary details of belief angered him. But the residue that he thought reasonable gave slight comfort to others, and there is little ground for supposing that in satisfying his own reason he fully satisfied his own soul. He might go on reiterating " righteousness " and " epieikia " for chapter after chapter, but there was little substance in it, no passion, and no vision. Marcus Aurelius himself, whose "religion" was not far from this, though still starker, has much more power of stirring the emotions ; such as it was, he held his faith with ardour. The phrases that Arnold coined with such facility were stock elements in serious journalism for a few decades, and now they are superseded by others. When he makes a deep appeal to his successors he makes it by his doubts in verse and not by his dogmas in prose, by his malady and not by his remedy, by his yearnings and not by his satisfactions. His literary criticism, though to some extent marred by his theories, is certainly alive, at least those parts of it are which deal with authors who are still read.

Chiefly, however, the great educational reformer of the 'sixties and the moralist of the 'seventies is to the modern reader a poet, a poet of the 'forties and 'fifties, a poet of melancholy, of regret, and of escape ; a grave, tender, sensitive poet, with a genius, at his best, for sad music and bright, remote pictures ; a man who remembered and lamented, and was bewildered. " Conduct, plain matter as it is, is six-eighths of life, while art and science are only two-eighths [he might have reduced his fractions] . . . That the world cannot get on without righteousness we have the clear experience, and a grand and admirable experience it is. . . . We who in this essay limit ourselves to experience, shall speak here of Christianity and of its greatness very soberly. Yet Christianity is really all the grander for that very reason which makes us speak about it in this sober manner—that it has such an immense development still before it." That is the tone of Arnold in the pulpit, of the Arnold whom conscience had compelled to get a doctrine of sorts ; he is cool and plausible, and always ready with a polished jibe if anybody objects. When the poet Arnold speaks it is with another voice :

> And the calm moonlight seems to say—
> " Hast thou then still the old unquiet breast ? "

He describes himself almost too insistently as—

> Wandering between two worlds, one dead,
> The other powerless to be born,
> With nowhere yet to rest my head . . .

In " Dover Beach " there is the same note, in a beautiful image :

> The sea of faith
> Was once, too, at the full, and round earth's shore
> Lay like the folds of a bright girdle furl'd.
> But now I only hear
> Its melancholy, long, withdrawing roar,
> Retreating, to the breath
> Of the night-wind, down the vast edges drear
> And naked shingles of the world.
>
> .   .   .   .   .   .
>
> And we are here as on a darkling plain
> Swept with confused alarms of struggle and flight
> Where ignorant armies clash by night.

In " Thyrsis " :

> Strange and vain the earthly turmoil grows
> And near and real the charm of thy repose,
> And night as welcome as a friend would fall—

and all the beautiful reminiscent pictures of the
" Scholar Gipsy " had to end with the old contrast ;
for that wanderer had been " free from the sick
fatigue, the languid doubt " of " we, Light half-
believers of our casual creeds, Who never deeply
felt, nor clearly willed." His doubt was a constant
preoccupation, his loneliness a recurrent pain ; and
the evidence of his poetry is confirmed by the
fascination, as subjects for poetry or criticism, exercised over him by two types of men, striving
solitaries harassed by life, and serene men who had
triumphed over it. When, as poet, he found peace,
it was commonly in some remote Arcadian picture,
drawn as often as not from a sunnier and simpler
ancient world. The postscript—it may have been
written earlier than the rest, but is certainly stuck
on—to the " Scholar Gipsy " is the most famous
and wonderful of these : a vision, or sequence of
visions :

> Then fly our greetings, fly our speech and smiles !
> As some grave Tynan trader, from the sea,
> Descried at sunrise an emerging prow,
> Lifting the cool-hair'd creepers stealthily,
> The fringes of a southward-facing brow
> Among the Aegean isles ;
> And saw the merry Grecian coaster come,
> Freighted with amber grapes, and Chian wine,
> Green bursting figs, and tunnies steep'd in brine ;
> And knew the intruders on his ancient home,
>
> The young light-hearted Masters of the waves ;
> And snatch'd his rudder, and shook out more sail,

> And day and night held out indignantly
> O'er the blue Midland waters with the gale,
> Betwixt the Syrtes and soft Sicily,
>   To where the Atlantic raves
> Outside the Western Straits, and unbent sails
>   There, where down cloudy cliffs, through
>   sheets of foam,
>   Shy traffickers, the dark Iberians come ;
> And on the beach undid his corded bales.

The picture of Cadmus and Harmonia is as well known :

> Far, far from here,
> The Adriatic breaks in a warm bay
> Among the green Illyrian hills ; and there
> The sunshine in the happy glens is fair,
> And by the sea, and in the brakes.
> The grass is cool, the sea-side air
> Buoyant and fresh, the mountain flowers
> As virginal and sweet as ours,
> And there, they say, two bright and aged snakes,
> Who once were Cadmus and Harmonia,
> Bask in the glens or on the warm sea-shore,
> In breathless quiet after all their ills.

When he is dwelling on pictures like these the poetry of Arnold breathes content. A joy more directly derived is very rare, but he had his moments :

> A bolt is shot back somewhere in our breast
> And a lost pulse of feeling stirs again :
> The eye sinks inward, and the heart lies plain,
> And what we mean, we say, and what we would,
>   we know.

MATTHEW ARNOLD

A man becomes aware of his life's flow
And hears its winding murmur, and he sees
The meadows where it glides, the sun, the breeze.
And there arrives a lull in the hot race
Wherein he doth for ever chase
That flying and elusive shadow, Rest.
An air of coolness plays upon his face,
And an unwonted calm pervades his breast.
And then he thinks he knows
The Hills where his life rose,
And the Sea where it goes.

It is temperate still ; introspection is not quite quenched ; " he thinks he knows." Yet it communicates a genuine emotion, and the pamphleteer Arnold, who talked as though he was sure he knew, did not.

He was a very considerable poet ; he had all the equipment to be a still greater one except the abiding certainty that poetry was better worth doing than anything else. At times one feels that he almost disapproves of poetry ; certainly in so far as it shares the nature of dance and Provençal song. A good deal of his work is dull, and some of it ungainly ; when he was not writing from a genuine impulse he often seemed, strangely, to lose his ear. The shrinkage of his poetical work was presumably due to his diversion, at the bidding of his sense of duty, to the task of saving civilisation ; some of his inferior verse is due to the same sense. He begins to think that the contribution of poetry to the discussion must be explicit. Poetry has often been inadequately defined, but seldom as inadequately as in his description of

95

it as a " criticism of life." If this definition be a true
one it was not worth making. He really might have
remembered some of his own best poems :

Children dear, was it yesterday
We heard the sweet bells over the bay ?
In the caverns where we lay,
Through the surf and through the swell
The far-off sound of a silver bell ?
Sand-strewn caverns, cool and deep,
Where the winds are all asleep ;
Where the spent lights quiver and gleam ;
Where the salt weed sways in the stream ;
Where the sea-beasts ranged all round
Feed in the ooze of their pasture-ground ;
Where the sea-snakes coil and twine,
Dry their mail and bask in the brine ;
Where great whales come sailing by,
Sail and sail, with unshut eye,
Round the word for ever and aye ?
When did music come this way ?
Children dear, was it yesterday ?

Of course it implies *something* ; you cannot ask a
man to open a window without implying that Life is
better with fresh air. If this be criticism a great many
people have been critics all their life without knowing it ; in fact, every infant lisps criticism. There
were times when this man who had written " simple,
sensuous, and passionate " verse, forgot it ; forgot
that he had even—temporarily and mistakenly—
suppressed " Empedocles on Etna " because, however
valid its " criticism of life," he thought it would

depress rather than delight, not leaving the reader that " balance of pleasure " which Wordsworth said should be produced by even the most tragic works of art.

Didacticism took possession of him, and possibly half the finest poetry he might have written he never wrote. He surrendered it in order to pursue the other aims of social service and the achievement of complete intellectual integrity, aims not less noble at all events. He served his time, and his loftiness of purpose was unquestionable. Fancy in a way came by her own ; in earnest as he was, he could never resist making his opponents look ridiculous ; from all his sermons peeps out an agile satirist who is the denied poet in another aspect. It might be said that, having deserted pure poetry because it was not serious enough, he became a social philosopher and preacher who scandalised people most of all by his brilliant levities. The most biting of them look very odd cheek by jowl with the appeals for " sweetness and light " and the solemnly iterated references to ·· the best that has been thought and said in the world."

ALICE MEYNELL

ALICE MEYNELL died last month. She was among the six or seven best women writers in the records of English literature, and the only one of them to achieve greatness as an essayist. Her first book was published in 1875, and was admired by Meredith, Ruskin and Rossetti. She did not publish a second for twenty years. A few more volumes of poems and essays followed. A collection of her worthiest prose was published under the title " Essays " in 1914, and she collected her poems in 1913. Those two volumes, with " Hearts of Controversy " (1919, a small collection of critical studies), a pamphlet of verse, and a few recent poems and papers, include all of her work which she wished to preserve.

It is, by modern standards, a small amount. Mrs. Meynell was never a professional writer, making daily recourse to a desk and producing books at regular intervals. She led an active and varied life. She bore and brought up a large family ; she read and travelled ; she entertained a large circle of friends ; and Francis Thompson, whose noble poem " Her Portrait " was inspired by her, was only the most conspicuous of many writers, particularly young ones, who went to her for counsel and encouragement. She lived as well as wrote, and she would not have chosen to do otherwise. Yet there was no question with her of writing in spare moments. She wrote when she felt inclined ; she spent great pains on preparation and revision ; she had no desire to produce a great body of work. It is not easy to conceive any alteration of circumstances—even that economic pressure which she was happily spared—which would have led her to write more profusely or less carefully ; and it may be assumed that what we have from her is all that she was born, or felt inclined, to give. By temperament and theory she was destined to do a few things as nearly perfectly as she could. Her philosophy was a kind of Christian stoicism, and she aimed at equanimity and self-control in her art as in her life.

There have been those whose careful and cunning artistry, tact and taste of expression, have arisen from a defect of passion. There was no defect of that in Alice Meynell ; she had much to control, and control never froze the springs of emotion in her. In old age she retained the quick sensitiveness of youth, sweet and generous impulses, instant responsiveness to cruelty and injustice. She was old when, in a poem to her sister, she described herself more surely than anyone else could.

> Our father works in us,
> The daughters of his manhood. Not undone
> Is he, not wasted, though transmuted thus,
> And though he left no son.

> Therefore on him I cry
> To arm me : " For my delicate mind a casque,
> A breastplate for my heart, courage to die,
> Of thee, captain, I ask.

" Nor strengthen only ; press
A finger on this violent blood and pale,
Over this rash will let thy tenderness
A while pause, and prevail.

" And shepherd-father, thou
Whose staff folded my thoughts before my birth,
Control them now I am of earth, and now
Thou art no more of earth."

Passionate feeling is expressed ; but the manner is
in conformity with the aspiration ; she will disclose
rather than proclaim. She detested and despised
the blatant expansiveness of the modern world, the
vulgar clamour, the sway of fashion, " the paltry
precipitancy of the multitude." There was nothing
of inhumanity in this, no feeling of superiority over
individuals unless they were brutal and base ; but it
did strengthen her aspiration and effort towards the
discipline and reticence to which she was naturally
inclined. There was never any risk that she should
turn herself into a machine ; she knew the inevitability and the value of impulse, the rare visitations
of vision and ecstasy ; she allowed scope to wilful
affection, to fine antipathies, even to harmless caprice.
Yet the central will was always operative. She was
not carried away. Her little releases and impetuosities
were, in her life and in her writings, like the vagrant
flowers that ran over the Roman arch in her Piranesi
print. She was strong and tender, reserved without
being cold, brave, scornful, compassionate ; and
she aimed at a balanced life, having an ideal of
deportment before God and man as complete as

were those of the old Renaissance writers who formulated codes of manners for Christian gentlemen.

Her character and her convictions are evident in every detail of her work. From beginning to end she laboured. She covertly defined her aim in an essay on " Innocence and Experience " :

> Perfect personal distinctness of Experience would be in literature a delicate Innocence. Not a passage of cheapness, of greed, of assumption, of sloth, or of any such sins in the work of him whose love-poetry were thus true, and whose *pudeur* of personality thus simple and inviolate. This is the private man, in other words the gentleman, who will neither love nor remember in common.

Writing (with marked originality) on Dr. Johnson's wife, she refuses to head the paper in the obvious way : " the chance of writing ' Tetty ' as a title is a kind of facile literary opportunity ; it shall be denied." To live up to the standard she had set herself meant an unremitting labour of observation, of analysis, of attention, of search : but she liked the labour. Walking unharnessed, she said, was easier than towing something : " So is the drawing of water in a sieve easier to the arms than drawing in a bucket, but not to the heart." The discipline of toil she sought with eagerness, and its results may be seen everywhere—in her initial conceptions as in her epithets. She would never write for the sake of writing, nor even where her interest was only ordinarily engaged. It was characteristic of her that when at last she published a small volume of critical studies she explained in a prefatory note that she would not have printed mere expositions or interpretations ; these comments were only made because important controversial issues were involved. Her criticisms are as independent as they could be ; every judgment, every word, is her own. That independence is evident in almost every poem and essay that she wrote, whether her theme was a commonplace theme suddenly perceived afresh or an unusual theme which had occurred to nobody before. Whatever mental or physical object or process she was contemplating was stripped of its conventional properties, examined anew, recorded with truth : she must see for herself and think for herself, and the results might be what they would. One effect of her independent and persistent habit of thought is that she was always making discoveries. She not merely saw familiar objects in an unaccustomed light, but she perceived novel relations between them. The situations and arguments she exhibits are sometimes so unusual as to give us the shock of oddity at first sight, but we soon become acclimatised to her truth. What a strange and beautiful thought it was—the mystery of Time governed much of her meditation—which made her in her girlhood write " A Letter from a Girl to Her own Old Age," in which she foresaw a time-worn woman touching the faded verses with thin fingers, and asked forgiveness of her :

> Pardon the girl ; such strange desires beset her.
> Poor woman, lay aside the mournful letter
> That breaks thy heart ; the one who wrote, forget
> her ;

ALICE MEYNELL

The one who now thy faded features guesses,
With filial fingers thy grey hair caresses,
With morning tears thy mournful twilight blesses.

She grew old ; she lived to read that from the other
end of the passage : to muse on the strange truth
of the girl who had envisaged her young self in a
daughterly relation to her older self. There is a parallel
strangeness in the recurring thought she had about
Dr. Johnson, whom perhaps she reverenced above any
other human being. He married a wife much older
than he, a wife unjustly treated by his biographers.
She predeceased him and he lived, cherishing her
memory, to grow older than she had been when her
senescence was arrested by death. " Time gave him,"
she wrote in an early essay, " a younger wife." When
near the last year of her life she returned to the idea
and linked it in a poem to a similar reflection on the
relation between herself and her own dead father :

Oh, by my filial tears
Mourned all too young, Father ! On this my head
Time yet will force at last the longer years,
Claiming some strange respect for me, from you,
the dead.

She writes, again, on the Shakespeare Tercentenary.
Only two writers—Mr. Thomas Hardy and Mrs.
Meynell—broke silence merely because they had
something to say. These were thinking about Shakespeare before they wrote. And Mrs. Meynell's reflections on the fact that she had lived through the
tercentenaries of Shakespeare's birth and death,

and might, with such a length of days, have seen him in his cradle and closed the earth on him, the image of that magnificence and fullness thus enclosed as it were within her own comparative waste (as she sees it), are very characteristic of her complete inability to write like a hack.

One may take another example. She has a poem on the Early Dead in Battle. But it is neither a lamentation over the young who have died before their prime, nor a thanksgiving that they died well. Her mind travels its own road, and she discovers to us, surprisingly but convincingly, that he who dies in early manhood has actually the *longest* part of life behind him, that time is never so long, and joy never so deep as in childhood, and that as we grow older our childhood seems a tract of almost immeasurable extent, but the later years much more fleeting and much less full :

What have you then foregone ?
A history ? This you had. Or memories ?
These, too, you had of your far distant dawn.
No further dawn seems his,

The old man who shares with you,
But has no more, no more. Time's mystery
Did once for him the most that it can do ;
He has had infancy.

And all his dreams, and all
His love for mighty Nature, sweet and few,
Are but the dwindling past he can recall
Of what his childhood knew.

He counts not any more
His brief, his present years. But oh, he knows
How far apart the summers were of yore,
How far apart the snows.

Therefore be satisfied
Long life is in your treasury ere you fall ;
Yes, and first love, like Dante's. O, a bride
For ever mystical !

Irrevocable good——
You dead, and now about, so young, to die,
Your childhood was, there Space, there Multitude,
There dwelt Antiquity.

Strangest, and most magnificent, of all the strange
thoughts upon which she came was that which is
expressed in " Christ in the Universe." She saw
mankind and our planet as citizens and a city in the
immeasurable Kingdom of the Universe ; and she
thought of the Redeemer carrying on His mission
in countless forms through the host of populous
stars :

No planet knows that this
Our wayside planet, carrying land and wave,
Love and life multiplied, and pain and bliss,
Bears, as chief treasure, one forsaken grave.

Nor, in our little day,
May his devices with the heavens be guessed,
His pilgrimage to thread the Milky Way,
Or his bestowals there be manifest.

But in the eternities,
Doubtless we shall compare together, hear,
A million alien Gospels, in what guise
He trod the Pleiades, the Lyre, the Bear. . . .

The pursuit of oddity for oddity's sake, the assumption of opinions because of their peculiarity, were, by the same token, and by virtue of her very honesty, even more nauseating to her than other kinds of falsity or pretence : her strangenesses are the direct results of her sincerity, and if she refused to " think in common," this did not mean that she disliked thoughts which other people shared. And the laborious sincerity of her more general meditations is observable in every process of her contemplation and of her art. She looked and looked at any thing, from a character to a chair, from a wandering thistledown to the night sky, until she had securely disengaged, in their order, all the impressions which she really received from it, as distinguished from those which other people had received from it or which it might be supposed to be incumbent upon her to receive. Examine this little jumble of her fresh impressions :

Suburbs divide a city from the fields as walls did never.

Much, too, of the spirit of time is lost to us because we will not let the sun rule the day. He would see to it that our hours were various ; but we have preferred to his various face the plain face of a clock, and the lights without vicissitudes of our nights without seasons.

The hiding-places that nature and the simpler crafts allot to the waters of wells are, at their deepest, in communication with the open sky. No other mine is so visited ; for the noonday sun himself is visible there ; and it is fine to think of the waters of this planet, shallow and profound, all charged with shining suns, a multitude of waters multiplying suns, and carrying that remote fire, as it were, within their unalterable freshness. Not a pool without this visitant, or without passages of stars.

Perhaps it will be found that to work all by day or all by night is to miss something of the powers of a complex mind.

All these things she discovered for herself. She had no desire to give to her own word " the common sanction of other men's summaries and conclusions." She went out whither she liked without bothering as to who had been there before, if anyone, or what had been said about it. So her freshnesses are perpetual, even when she is on the commonest ground. Looking at the electric light, clear and clean, she discovers it to be as beautiful as any light. Looking at the streaks of rain which are really rapidly moving drops, she muses : " There seems to be such a difference of instants as invests all swift movement with mystery in man's eyes, and causes the past, a movement of old, to be written, vanishing, upon the skies." And walking abroad, meditating on our habit of brooding over Nature's cruelty, and the death and destruction with which air, earth and water are filled, it suddenly occurs to her to notice " the suppression

of death and of the dead " throughout the landscape
of manifest life. " Where," she asks, " are they—
all the dying, all the dead, of the populous woods ?
Where do they hide their little last hours, where are
they buried ? Where is the violence concealed ?
Under what gay custom and decent habit ? "

That same concentration, that same passion for
exactitude which governed what she said, also con-
trolled and directed every phase of her expression.
She aimed at the utmost possible precision of statement. She began, as it were, by a long and hard look
at the objects of her observation, endeavouring to
reach and define their dominant qualities as they
appeared to her vision. The material world was alive
to her ; everything was alive and active ; it was
something, and it was doing something. Within
colour and form there was purpose and function,
growth and resistance. She defined the characters
of trees, houses and walls as subtly and sympathetic-
ally as if they were the characters of human beings ;
and the qualities in them, so sought and found,
could only be described in terms used of human
qualities. Some of her finest essays are inspired
entirely by the characters of things. There is " The
Sea-Wall," where she states the whole strength and
majesty of the stone against the sea : " the wall,
steadying its slanting foot upon the rock, builds in
the serried ilex-wood and builds out the wave."
More beautiful still is " Ceres' Runaway," where
the three sets of characters are the venerable and
kindly walls, churches and ruins of antiquity, the
laughing flowers and grasses that clamber over them,
the despairing municipality that vainly chases the

flowers. They are all seized with a delicious precision : the " agile fugitive safe on the arc of a flying buttress," the running " importunate " grass, the church that is " full of attitude," and " can hardly be aware that a crimson snapdragon of great stature and many stalks and blossoms is standing on its furthest summit tiptoe against the sky." She distinguishes the generic and individual qualities of reeds and seeds, clouds, waters and winds ; and having distinguished them proceeds, with unremitted continuity of labour, to search for the closest possible words, making deletion after deletion in the mind or on paper. No writer has had a more exquisite sense of the value of words, their shades of meaning and their associative, evocative qualities. When she was satisfied she had reason to be satisfied : in her best passages no word could be improved, none could be added or subtracted without loss. For her ideal of precision carried with it a necessity of the most rigid economy. She was never vaguely impressionistic. Where brief suggestion would do the work she used it. She is standing for example on a low shore and looking out over the marine waste : the whole scene is called up by the bare sentence : " You can see the wave as far as you can see the water." Where detail had to be mentioned to give the impression required it was mentioned as sparingly, and with as small a measure of epithet, as was consonant with the communication of the picture ; her scenes are as clear and as thriftily indicated as the best landscapes of Mr. Bridges. How she corrected and compressed may be certainly known from the only passage which occurs in two of her essays.

" Innocence and Experience " contains this comparison :

> As the Franciscans wear each other's old habits, and one friar goes about darned because of another's rending, so the poet of a certain order grows cynical for the sake of many poets' old loves. Not otherwise will the resultant verse succeed in implying so much—or rather so many, in the feminine plural. The man of very sensitive individuality might hesitate at the adoption. The Franciscan is understood to have a fastidiousness and to overcome it. And yet, if choice were, one might wish rather to make use of one's fellowmen's old shoes than put their old secrets to use, and dress one's art in a motley of past passions.

It reappears, amended, pruned, stiffened, in the article on Swinburne :

> As one friar goes darned for another's rending, having no property in cassock and cowl, so does many a poet, not in humility, but in a paradox of pride, boast of the past of others. And yet, one might rather choose to make use of one's fellowmen's old shoes than to put their old secrets to usufruct, and dress poetry in a motley of shed passions, twice corrupt.

It is shorter now ; there is an added touch of the concrete ; an almost unnoticeable verbal repetition has gone ; a touch of archaism has been removed from the rhythm of the final phrase, of which, simultaneously, the meaning has been strengthened. That, ultimately, was her object : to marry economy with music. Euphony must be secured with no loss of accuracy : without padding, and without the loose employment of any of those words, the incommunicables and everlastings, with which artificers of prose so commonly secure themselves a ready-made melody. In her criticism of Swinburne's " fundamental fumbling," his " paltry, shaky and unvisionary " images, his reckless scattering of the stock picturesque and the stock musical words, may be seen the reflection of her own theory and practice.

The fruit of all these labours is a style, personal without parade of personality, beautiful without parade of ornament, a style at its best approaching perfection. What is this prose like, I wonder ? It is like a bell ; or it is like a clear spring country ; or it is like a strong pear tree, pruned and nailed to the wall, its firm symmetrical branches full of sap and covered with blossom ; at one moment or another it seems like each of these. Mrs. Meynell's prose is always clear ; where her verse is at first sight difficult it is only so from the rapid flight of her thought. She had few mannerisms ; an excessive fondness for a certain company of euphonious words, such as " uncovenanted " and "alien," may be noted as the chief of them. Nor are echoes, traces of derivation, often encountered in her work. No essayist altogether avoids falling at times into the accents of a previous essayist. When, very rarely, another voice mingles with Mrs. Meynell's it is seldom the elsewhere ubiquitous accents of the Lambs and the Hazlitts that we hear, but the older tones of Bacon. They are here, in the sentence previously quoted :

And yet, if choice were, one might wish rather to make use of one's fellow-men's old shoes than put their old secrets to use, and dress one's art in a motley of past passions.

The affinity was natural with Bacon, whose prose was so frugal and close, and yet so beautiful ; but if sometimes she borrowed a shape the content was always hers still. Usually her prose, free though it was from tricks, was unmistakably hers, and incontrovertibly good. It was, as was inevitable when a passion for accuracy and compression was united with a fastidious ear, fertile in striking and charming phrases. Discussing the raving tragedies of the time, she says " The eighteenth century stuck straws in its periwig " ; such felicities came to her easily. With her, however, they grew out of their contexts ; she was no phrase-maker in the ordinary sense, though many of her best passages are webs of good phrases. Sentences which linger in the memory for their music are also common, sentences like :

No richer scents throng each other, close and warm, than these from a little hand-space of the grass one rests on, within the walls or on the plain, or in the Sabine or the Alban hills.

Her openings always are especially notable for decision of sense and sound. Here is one, characteristic :

There are hours claimed by Sleep, but refused to him. None the less are they his by some state within the mind, which answers rhythmically and punctually to that claim. Awake and at work, without drowsiness, without languor and without gloom, the night mind of man is yet not his day mind ; he has night-powers of feeling which are at their highest in dreams, but are night's as well as sleep's. The powers of the mind in dream, which are inexplicable, are not altogether baffled because the mind is awake ; it is the hour of their return as it is the hour of a tide's, and they do return.

Here is another, less grave :

The world at present is inclined to make sorry mysteries or unattractive secrets of the methods and supplies of the fresh and perennial means of life. A very dull secret is made of water, for example, and the plumber sets his seal upon the floods whereby we live. They are covered, they are carried, they are hushed, from the spring to the tap ; and when their voices are released at last in the London scullery, why it can hardly be said that the song is eloquent of the natural source of waters, whether earthly or heavenly. There is not one of the circumstances of this capture of streams—the company, the water-rate, and the rest—that is not a sign of the ill-luck of modern devices in regard to style. For style implies a candour and simplicity of means, an action, a gesture, as it were, in the doing of small things ; it is the ignorance of secret ways ; whereas the finish of modern life and its neatness seem to be secured by a system of little shufflings and surprises.

This is light ; it has the touch of humour, almost subcutaneous, which was all she usually allowed herself. Many moods she did not permit herself, many effects she never aimed at ; all she tried she did with perfect efficiency. Her powers of simple evocation and of exact and full description may be illustrated by two more extracts. The first is from the essay on the Brontës. She is talking of the bareness which marks the greatest moments in literature :

> The student passes delighted through the several courts of poetry, from the outer to the inner, from riches to more imaginative riches, and from decoration to more complex decoration ; and prepares himself for the greater opulence of the innermost chamber. But when he crosses the last threshold he finds this midmost sanctuary to be a hypæthral temple, and in its custody and care a simple earth and a space of sky.

The other occurs in a beautiful piece which came from watching the stars reflected in a dark pool of a river. The deep water moved and was still :

> The flood lets a constellation fly, as Juliet's " wanton " with a tethered bird, only to pluck it home again. At moments some rhythmic flux of the water seems about to leave the darkly-set, widely-spaced Bear absolutely at large, to dismiss the great stars, and refuse to imitate the skies, and all the water is obscure ; then one broken star returns, then fragments of another, and a third and a fourth flit back to their noble places,

brilliantly vague, wonderfully visible, mobile, and unalterable. There is nothing else at once so keen and so elusive.

The aspen poplar had been in captive flight all day, but with no such vanishings as these. The dimmer constellations of the soft night are reserved by the skies. Hardly is a secondary star seen by the large and vague eyes of the stream. They are blind to the Pleiades.

Mrs. Meynell's work had its limitations. She was aware of them, and some of them were imposed by her own will. She was one kind of writer and not another kind : an admiration for her does not preclude a still greater admiration for more voluminous artists like Dickens and more careless artists like Shakespeare. None of her writings is long : her aim was to compress all she could into a lyric or a few pages of prose, inspired by a thing seen and deeply felt or by some flash of vision into the ways of life. She never made the slightest effort to adapt herself to an audience ; she would not withhold her knowledge, or modify her vocabulary, or win attention by facile confidences. She had a great passion for Dr. Johnson, but she could not have borne to brandish a bludgeon herself. She loved Falstaff and the broadest pages of Dickens, but her own works might be searched in vain for a single sentence which might be termed rollicking. Her humour was not, and could not be, entirely concealed : but she preferred to smile rather than to laugh. " It may be," she remarks, " no more than a brief perversity that has set a number of our writers to cheer the memory of Charles II. Perhaps, even, it is no more than another rehearsal of that untiring success at the expense of the bourgeois. . . . The bourgeois would be more simple than he is were he to stand up every time to be shocked; but, perhaps, the mere image of his dismay is enough to reward the fancy of those who practise the wanton art." How charmingly economical ! How flickering, again, the smile which plays over her lips as she describes the obsession of modern man with the flower as a decoration !

Stem and petal and leaf—the fluent forms that a man has not by heart but certainly by rote—are woven, printed, cast, and stamped wherever restlessness and insimplicity have feared to leave plain spaces. The most ugly of all imaginable rooms, which is probably the parlour of a farmhouse arrayed for those whom Americans call summerboarders, is beset with flowers. It blooms, a dry, woollen, papery, cast-iron garden. The floor flourishes with blossoms adust, poorly conventionalised into a kind of order ; the table-cover is ablaze with a more realistic florescence ; the wallpaper is set with bunches ; the rigid machinelace curtain is all of roses and lilies in its very construction ; over the muslin blinds an impotent sprig is scattered. In the worsted rosettes of the bell-ropes, in the plaster picture-frames, in the painted tea-tray and on the cups, in the pediment of the sideboard, in the ornament that crowns the barometer, in the finials of sofa and armchair, in the finger-plates of the " grained " door, is to be seen the ineffectual portrait or to be traced the stale inspiration of the flower. And what is this bossiness around the grate but some blunt, black-leaded garland ?

That was her way—the way of quietness and moderation. She moved " in captive flight " like her own aspen. Inclination and theory reinforced each other : she was inclined that way, and a decivilised world needed examples of restraint and care. One says a " world " ; but she had no illusions about the narrowness of her direct appeal. She was writing with all the veracity of which she was capable, and using, consequently, all the education she possessed and every response she felt : the result was naturally a product only to be completely understood and appreciated by a public which was accustomed to fine distinctions, which would not miss her frequent allusions, and which could relish the precision of her language. What influence she could exercise would be chiefly indirect ; it could not be helped, and she had no hankering at all for a more public platform. For all her restraint and her pains of craftsmanship, however, expression always remained a means to her. What she wished to say still remained the dominant thing : the instrument was an instrument to an end. Here she differed in a marked degree from some of those moderns who have set themselves to make " emaux et camées," and who have ended by worshipping the picture, the cadence, and the word. Her style never became a Narcissus admiring himself in a pool. Casual readers sometimes thought her " precious " ; no careful reader possibly could. She loathed the slipshod, but she regarded meretricious ornament with equal disgust ; she refused to use a loose word but she disdained to use an affected word ; under her firm surface was the fire of humanity. And what any careful reader must soon discover, the person who knew her could not but perceive at first sight. I, one of many who were honoured by her kindness and benefited by her wisdom, shall carry her gracious memory to the grave. There, in her London flat or in the ample library-living room of her country cottage, she would sit in her corner : a woman with unwhitened hair, very erect and calm : " straight as a stalk of lavender " was Coventry Patmore's phrase. Her skin was withered with age, but her eyes were large and lustrous : at seventy she still gave an impression of youth and beauty. She was usually in black, her only little coquetry a velvet ribbon around her neck. She sat quiet, Roman dignity in her mien, vivacity, feeling, mockery, sympathy in her eyes : a saint and a sibyl smoking a cigarette : with a young girl's sensitiveness, an old woman's insight, a man's strength. She listened tolerantly to conversation, but flashed at a word of brutality. Her own remarks were brief : wise, humorous, full of "the scorn of scorn, the hate of hate, the love of love." She swooped on the essentials of a character like a hawk on a bird, but she pitied every bird. She detested vulgarity and cruelty ; she excused ignorance. At the back of all her judgments, invariably convincing, was a mind not merely exquisitely discriminating, but uninterruptedly aware of the unseen behind the seen. She, a religious ascetic, practised " art for art's sake " as ruthlessly as any despairing hedonist of them all ; and, naturally fastidious, she had no tinge of niceness or superiority. She was proud to the world, but humble before goodness ; she enjoyed small things, but the universe was behind them all. There is a sentence in Bacon's " Advancement of Learning " which runs thus :

> So certainly, if a man meditate upon the universal frame of nature, the earth with men upon it, the divineness of souls excepted, will not seem much other than an ant-hill, where some ants carry corn, and some carry their young, and some go empty, and all to and fro on a little heap of dust.

Swift cultivated this detached " meditation " for one motive, Anatole France for another. " The divineness of souls excepted " is a large reservation, and, with Mrs. Meynell, so large that it almost cancels the rest. Almost, but not altogether. She too, after her manner, retires into the immensities of Time and Space and looks at pain and pleasure, birth and death, as small and transient things : not for perverse amusement or the consciousness of superiority, but for a consolation and a refuge. Contemplation of the large processes of life and the mysteries of eternity was habitual with her, and moved her at intervals to the grandest and most sustained of her passages. None of these, I think, is grander than that in which she concludes her investigation of the strange regularity which permeates all things, which governs the motions of the planets and drives men to write verse :

It has been found that several tribes in Africa and in America worship the moon and not the sun ; a great number worship both ; but no tribes are known to adore the sun and not the moon. On her depend the tides ; and she is Selene, mother of Herse, bringer of the dews that recurrently irrigate lands where rain is rare. More than any other companion of earth she is the Measurer. Early Indo-Germanic languages knew her by that name. Her metrical phases are the symbol of the order of recurrence. Constancy in approach and in departure is the reason of her inconstancies. Juliet will not receive a vow spoken in invocation of the moon ; but Juliet did not live to know that love itself has tidal times—lapses and ebbs which are due to the metrical rule of the interior heart, but which the lover vainly and unkindly attributes to some outward alteration in the beloved. For man—except those elect already named—is hardly aware of periodicity. The individual man either never learns it fully, or learns it late. And he learns it so late, because it is a matter of cumulative experience upon which cumulative evidence is long lacking. It is in the after-part of each life that the law is learnt so definitely as to do away with the hope or fear of continuance. That young sorrow comes so near to despair is a result of this young ignorance. So is the early hope of great achievement. Life seems so long, and its capacity so great, to one who knows nothing of all the intervals it needs must hold and the intervals between aspirations, between actions, pauses as inevitable as the pauses of sleep. And life looks impossible to the young unfortunate, unaware of the inevitable and unfailing refreshment. It would be for their peace to learn that there is a tide in the affairs of men, in a sense more subtle—if it is not too audacious to add a meaning to Shakespeare—than the phrase was meant to contain. Their joy is flying away from them on its way home ; their life will wax and wane ; and if they would be wise they must wake and rest in its phases, knowing that they are ruled by the law that commands all things—a sun's revolutions and the rhythmical pangs of maternity.

Meredith said of her essays : " They leave a sense of stilled singing in the mind they fill." Here, as in a few other passages where she allowed herself to be moved to a sustained eloquence, it is a deeper vibration that dies upon the air. It is the echoing end of an organ music.

MR. ROBERT BRIDGES'S LYRICAL POEMS*

I

MR. BRIDGES'S new volume of poems (the first that he has published since he became Poet Laureate) must be read for what it is, the work of a man seventy-five years of age. This statement is not made as an excuse : there are weak—occasional and patriotic—poems in the book, but some also which are beautiful additions to his canon. But some of his critics, so inadequate is still the recognition of what he has done, have treated the book as though his claim to be a great poet rested partly upon it, failing to read it, as they should, in the light of all that has gone before it. Properly regarded, it awakes not disappointment, but wonder that a poet so old should still sometimes have the genuine impulse, should still keep his spirit fresh, and should still be capable of ingenious and fruitful experiments in technique—experiments moreover in which the content is never subordinated to the form, however exacting and interesting the form may be. " October," " Noel," " Our Lady," " Flycatchers," " The West Front," " Trafalgar Square," and " Fortunatus Nimium " are all poems that any man might be proud to write in his prime ; and beyond these there is the delicious invention of " The Flowering Tree " :

* "October and Other Poems." By Robert Bridges. Heinemann. 1920. "Poetical Works, excluding the Eight Dramas." By Robert Bridges. 1912. Oxford University Press.

MR. ROBERT BRIDGES'S LYRICAL POEMS

What Fairy fann'd my dreams
    while I slept in the sun ?
As if a flowering tree
    were standing over me :
Its young stem strong and lithe
    went branching overhead,
And willowy sprays around
    fell tasselling to the ground
All with wild blossom gay
    as is the cherry in May . . .

The sunlight was enmesh'd
    in the shifting splendour
And I saw through on high
    to soft lakes of blue sky : . . .

So I slept enchanted
    under my loving tree
Till from his late resting
    the sweet songster of night,
Rousing, awakened me :
    Then ! this—the birdis note—
Was the voice of thy throat
    which thou gav'st me to kiss.

The occasion may suitably be seized to make a few
notes on Mr. Bridges's shorter — never mind the
title and the word " lyrical "—poems as a whole.

II

Mr. Bridges is often written of as though he were
primarily a technician. He has always taken a keen
interest in prosody ; he has written books, and

formulated theories, about it ; his experiments in classical metres and his notions about English spelling have, to those who have not troubled to discover the intellectual strength and the strong common sense which commonly marks his linguistic writings, given him something of the air of a pedant. But the theoriser and the innovator of the " shorter poems " has nothing to do with pedantry. There are poems in which the scrutinous eye may detect very elaborate pains. " April 1885 " is a complicated fabric of internal rhyme, assonance, and alliteration which it would be hard to parallel in English :

Wanton with long delay the gay Spring leaping
    cometh ;
The blackthorn starreth now his bough on the eve
    of May :
All day in the sweet box-tree the bee for pleasure
    hummeth :
The cuckoo sends afloat his note on the air all day.

Now dewy nights again and rain in gentle shower
At root of tree and flower have quenched the winter's
    drouth :
On high the hot sun smiles, and banks of cloud up-
    tower
In bulging heads that crowd for miles the dazzling
    south.

That may be called a *tour-de-force* ; as a rule, though Mr. Bridges's variety of stanza and rhythm is immense, the craftsman never intrudes. His ingenuities merely serve their purpose ; his music cannot be separated from his sense ; his rhythms are sought, and found, as the only suitable rhythms for the words and the scenes that are being expressed and described. How otherwise than in the beautiful movement he uses can we imagine the picture of " A Passer By " ? —the fresh blue day, the crowded sail, the vision of a queenly progress across the world to a far har- bour in the south ? It is one of fifty such feats, triumphs of fastidious art, never completely under- stood until the poems are read aloud. His power of music has developed steadily throughout his career, but scarcely a poem of any period can be quoted without illustrating his surpassing technical gifts. We shall come to many presently ; here, when we are thinking primarily of the skill with which he weaves a close-fitting garment of sound for his thought, we may take as a single example, " London Snow " :

When men were all asleep the snow came flying,
In large white flakes falling on the city brown,
Stealthily and perpetually settling and loosely lying,
　　Hushing the latest traffic of the drowsy town,
Deadening, muffling, stifling its murmurs failing ;
Lazily and incessantly floating down and down ;
　　Silently sifting and veiling road, roof, and railing ;
Hiding difference, making unevenness even,
Into angles and crevices softly drifting and sailing.
　　All night it fell, and when full inches seven
It lay in the depth of its uncompacted lightness,
The clouds blew off from a high and frosty heaven. . .

The accuracy of the description is extraordinary and

continues as the town awakes, and boys go snow-
balling to school, a few carts creak along, and the
pale sun rises to awake the noisier day. But the
observation, the accuracy, the response of the heart
to the beauty of the scene, might have been found
elsewhere : the astonishing management of the
rhythms, which, even when divorced from the meaning of the words, translate the steady falling, the
wayward criss-crossing, the lightness and crispness,
and soothing persistence of snow in an almost wind-
less air, is peculiar to Mr. Bridges. Words and music
are with him always inseparable : he is at the opposite
pole from the man, often not unintelligent in other
ways, who forces his material into a strait-jacket of
jingle. In this respect his taste is as flawless, his
subtlety as unfailing, as any in the records of literature.

III

It is possible, and it has often been stated, that
Mr. Bridges will chiefly live as a poet of the English
landscape. Certainly he would live if only his landscape poetry were preserved. It may seem a large
assertion, but no Englishman has written so large a
body of good landscape poetry. There are two obvious
things to be said about it.

The first is that his landscape is the landscape of
the South of England, more particularly of the
Thames Valley and the downs by the sea—two
regions which he significantly chooses as typical,
when, in " The Voice of Nature," he wishes to point
an argument. He never describes foreign or remote

scenes ; and—it may be regarded as symbolic of his attitude to the more violent things of life—he never leaves the land for the sea. Even British territorial waters he never sails ; there is much of the sea in his work, but it is the sea as seen from the shore, blue and smiling and dancing, or whipped by the wind, caught in a narrow peep between shoulders of the downs or watched from a hill through a telescope :

There many an hour I have sat to watch ; nay, now
The brazen disk is cold against my brow,
And in my sight a circle of the sea
Enlarged to swiftness, where the salt waves flee,
And ships in stately motion pass so near
That what I see is speaking to my ear.

Mr. Bridges's landscape is bounded by the English Channel ; his hills are the Downs ; his rivers are clear and gentle streams ; his trees oak and beech, elm and larch ; he is as surely of the South of England as Wordsworth is of the North. And the second obvious thing is that, being a true landscape poet and not a romantic who exploits nature to find backgrounds for his passions, it is of ordinary landscapes that he writes. Tennyson, too, was an observer, but many of his best-known landscapes are of the selected kind. It is one thing to write of the sort of natural scene traditionally approved as remarkable : sunset on a marsh, sunrise on the Alps, stupendous cliffs, high cataracts, and breakers in the moon. It is another to describe, giving the breath of life to your description, what any man, going out on any day in any season, will see when he looks over a five-barred gate or takes a footpath through the woods. Mr. Bridges writes of nature like a countryman. Compared with Clare's or Mr. Blunden's his observation is that of an inspired country gentleman as against that of an inspired farmer's boy : but it is just as genuine and just as close as theirs. His abnormal scenes are rare; he sees the beauty in the normal. He sings of nightingales when he hears them, but rooks are far more frequent in his verse ; his suns seldom go down in flaming splendour, but drop red into the grey or die invisibly. One by one scenes from his familiar landscape have moved him to verse, until his books contain a complete catalogue of the English rural year, all its ordinary recurrent colours, and scents and sounds, trees, flowers, birds, skies and waters.

Spring. A village in the downs, and men winnowing in a barn. The palm-willows and hazels. The first flowers, primroses and green hyacinth spikes, shooting up amid moss and withered undergrowth. Brisk ploughmen. Birds happily courting in the jocund sun.

Summer. The garden, with bees on the flowers and in the overhanging limes, and rooks cawing in the elms. The hayfields in the sun ; fields green with waves of rustling wheat ; the hum of insects and the song of larks in a sky pure blue, or heaped with " slow pavilions of caverned snow," " sunshot palaces of cloud " ; the downs, starred with small flowers, where rabbits nibble the grass ; the noise of scythes. The river : still water, the dip of oars, a boat that glides with its reflection past flowering islets and dipping branches and meadows, where " the lazy cows wrench many a scented flower " ; bathers ; fish leaping in the pools ; the peace of evening as it falls over water and trees ; moonlight on the flashing weir. There are storms that blacken the sea and beat down the corn, but they pass and the sun comes out again, gathering strength.

Autumn. The garden in September, with late flowers. The ripe orchards and fields where " the sun spots the deserted gleanings with decay." The winds of October that come and fill ruts and pools with golden leaves. The later storms that mingle the leaves with snow.

Winter. The short days and the infrequent sun on lonely songless lands. Rooks after the plough, the team against the skyline. A rough sea and snow on the beach. Robin on the leafless bough. Dark afternoons and evenings by the fire, companioned or alone.

All those signs of the seasons and hundreds more could be illustrated from Mr. Bridges. One cannot do more here than huddle together a few characteristic fragments from which the whole may be deduced. If the first three are records of the shape, colour and movement of clouds, it is fitting : all Mr. Bridges's landscapes have skies, and most of his skies (being English) have clouds :

From distant hills their shadows creep,
    Arrive in turn and mount the lea,
And flit across the downs and leap
    Sheer off the cliff upon the sea ;

And sail and sail far out of sight.
But still I watch their fleecy trains,
That piling all the south with light,
Dapple in France the fertile plains. . . .

And o'er the treetops, scattered in mid-air,
The exhausted clouds laden with crimson light
Floated, or seemed to sleep ; and, highest there,
One planet broke the lingering ranks of night. . . .

The upper skies are palest blue
Mottled with pearl and fretted snow :
With tattered fleece of inky hue
Close overhead the storm-clouds go.

Their shadows fly along the hill
And o'er the crest mount one by one :
The whitened planking of the mill
Is now in shade and now in sun. . . .

With gentle flaws the western breeze
Into the garden saileth,
Scarce here and there stirring the single trees,
For his sharpness he vaileth :
So long a comrade of the bearded corn
Now from the stubbles whence the shocks are borne,
O'er dewy lawns he turns to stray,
As mindful of the kisses and soft play
Wherewith he enamoured the light-hearted May,
Ere he deserted her ;
Lover of fragrance, and too late repents ;
Nor more of heavy hyacinth now may drink,
Nor spicy pink,

Nor summer's rose, nor garnered lavender,
But the few lingering scents
Of streakèd pea, and gillyflower and stocks
Of courtly purple and aromatic phlox.

And at all times to hear are drowsy tones
Of dizzy flies, and humming drones,
With sudden flap of pigeon wings in the sky,
Or the wild cry
Of thirsty rooks, that scour ascare
The distant blue, to watering as they fare
With creaking pinions, or—on business bent,
If aught their ancient polity displease—
Come gathering to their colony, and there
Settling in ragged parliament,
Some stormy council hold in the high trees. . . .

In the golden glade the chestnuts are falling all ;
From the sered boughs of the oak the acorns fall ;
The beech scatters her ruddy fire ;
The lime has stripped to the cold,
And standeth naked above her yellow attire ;
The larch thinneth her spire
To lay the ways of the wood with cloth of gold.
Out of the golden-green and white
Of the brake the fir-trees stand upright
In the forest of flame, and wave aloft
To the blue of heaven their blue-green tuftings soft. . . .

Out by the ricks the mantled engine stands
Crestfallen, deserted—for now all hands
Are told to the plough—and ere it is dawn appear
The teams following and crossing far and near,

As hour by hour they broaden the brown bands
Of the striped fields ; and behind them firk and
      prance
The heavy rooks, and daws grey-pated dance :
As awhile, surmounting a crest, in sharp outline
(A miniature of toil, a gem's design)
They are pictured, horses and men, or now near by
Above the lane they shout lifting the share,
By the trim hedgerow bloom'd with purple air. . . .

The long dark night, that lengthens slow,
Deepening with Winter to starve grass and tree,
And soon to bury in snow
The Earth, that, sleeping 'neath her frozen stole,
Shall dream a dream crept from the sunless pole
Of how her end shall be.

The best of all (such as " The Downs " and " The
Storm is Over ") cannot be quoted except entirely ;
they are landscapes complete, earth and sky. But
let it not be supposed that Mr. Bridges is ever a mere
describer who sits down mechanically in front of
any scene with his little box of water-colours. We
have known such, and sometimes they have been
learned in botany ; their exactitude of detail is dull,
their serried statements useless ; only the man who
is touched by the beauty in a scene, or aroused by a
scene to an awareness of beauty behind it, will fuse
the several things he sees into a whole. The writer
who has felt no emotion communicates none, and
the greatness of Mr. Bridges's poems of landscape
is derived not solely from his knowledge of landscape, the wary eye, but from his feeling for it, the

eye of love. His scenes are precise, but they are never photographs ; there is no doubt about the sentiment that he felt when he saw them.

IV

And Mr. Bridges, even when at his best, is not only a landscape poet, but a poet cunning in the experiences of the heart. Very many of his poems are love poems and many of them are beautiful : if the fact has not been widely observed it must be because they are happy love poems, or at least because they are not excessive in expression. The proclivity that makes him, in another sphere, write not about storms but about calms after storms, is seen always : he has no violence, no vehement abandonment. But there is little of that in Wordsworth and other poets the depth of whose affections, the reality of whose suffering, cannot be doubted. Mr. Bridges's love-poetry makes no brutal assault on us. His constant reference to Virgil, Mozart and the old composers is significant. He never declaims, never raves, despairs, or burns in print : but he knows the ways of lovers' hearts, and his quiet stanzas, whether their subject be the pain of doubt, or separation, or the joy of union, or calm affection by the warm domestic hearth, have a truth and strength which outwear the ardours of many poets. In " When My Love was Away," " My Spirit sang all day," " I will not let thee go," and twenty more the lover's calendar is written as that of the seasons elsewhere, and if his praise is soft and measured like the old music in which he so constantly delights, love's fine extravagance is, for all the tempered sound, nevertheless there :

> Her beauty would surprise
> Gazers on Autumn eves,
> Who watched the broad moon rise
> Upon the scattered sheaves.

He is self-controlled and never shouts ; he does not hunt the universe for new and strange sorrows nor harrow himself overmuch with the problems of existence ; but those griefs that fall to the common lot of mankind have come to him and drawn beautiful poetry from him. Many poets have written habitually of Death ; few have said as little about Death as Mr. Bridges ; but he has said all he has to say and need say about death, loss, and sorrow in two poems, the poem which begins :

> I never shall love the snow again
> Since Maurice died,

and the other " On a Dead Child " : " Perfect little body, without fault or stain on thee . . . ."

> So I lay thee there, thy sunken eyelids closing—
>> Go lie thou there in thy coffin, thy last little bed—
> Propping thy wise, sad head,
> Thy firm, pale hands across thy chest disposing.

So quiet ! doth the change content thee ?—Death,
    whither hath he taken thee ?
To a world, do I think, that rights the disaster
    of this ?
The vision of which I miss,
Who weep for the body, and wish but to warm thee
    and awaken thee ?

Ah ! little at best can all our hopes avail us
    To lift this sorrow, or cheer us, when in the
    dark,
    Unwilling, alone we embark,
And the things we have seen and have known and
    have heard of, fail us.

In " Winter Nightfall " there is all the complaint
of ailing old age, in " Pater Filio " the passionate
anxiety of parent for child ; the normal, inevitable
griefs and dejections are all here, expressed with
gravity, yet always with poignancy. But normal and
inevitable they are. One gets the impression that,
beyond the " common lot," the poet has had few
distresses. Intense joy—nobody has given it better
definition than he—is as rare as intense sadness,
but ordinarily he is happy, or at worst not uncom-
fortably melancholy, and the happiness has become
more pervasive as he has grown older. He is the poet
of a leisured country life, led by a sensitive physically
healthy man, with whom the major things of life
have gone well and who, in those circumstances, is
temperamentally inclined to a grateful contentment.

V

Mr. Bridges has not made the easy appeal by violence of expression ; and he has not made the easy appeal by violence of doctrine. If he has been less discussed than many inferior writers, it is not so much that he is without doctrine as that he is without novel doctrine and has never been a doctrinaire. Any noisy demonstrator with a new lie may attract attention, if it is only the attention of those who wish to dispute with him ; and it is easier to dispute (or agree) with the man whose " views " are explicit than with him who leaves them implicit. The mere fact that Mr. Bridges's practical philosophy has been held by hundreds of millions of ordinary people in many ages does not prove that he has no philosophy. He is a Christian, but he says little about that. He is politically sceptical of systems, but he says little about that. He accepts life, with its pains and pleasures, and he is happy that his life has been cast in an ordered traditional civilisation. He sees life in proportion, with the greater goods clear : childhood, the love of a woman and of children, the beauty of the earth, days of peace, joyful work, friendship. He does not proclaim a way of life, but it will be easy for his critics to deduce one from his poetry : if he does not tell people how to enjoy life it is because is he too busy enjoying it himself, and if he does not expound his religion, it is because he probably holds it to be " the religion of all sensible men." He never loses hold of his settled philosophy. In depression he does not imaginatively

revel in the gloom of a Universe gone black, but
consoles himself out of his knowledge :

> O soul, be patient : thou shalt find
> A little matter mend all this,
> Some strain of music to thy mind,
> Some praise for skill not spent amiss.

In the peace of a churchyard he can write :

Nay, were my last hope quenched, I here would sit
And praise the annihilation of the pit.

He lives through the moments of dejection and
awaits, with sure hope, those moments when

> Life and joy are one—we know not why—
> As though our very blood long breathless lain
> Had tasted of the breath of God again.

There are times when he is at almost that pitch of
bliss for days together, and he says with each evening :

> That I have known no day
> In all my life like this.

And with any dawn may come the exhilaration and
the resolve

> I too will something make
> And joy in the making.

Very rarely some slight dogmatic statement is actually present, the affirmation of something which is
not necessarily false because it is as old as man, and

modestly put. " For howsoe'er man hug his care, The best of his art is gay." He sees Spring in Winter more often than Winter in Spring :

> And God the Maker doth my heart make bold
> To praise for writing works not understood,
> Who all the worlds and ages doth behold,
> Evil and good as one, and all as good.

It may by some be called an easy acceptance ; by others the answer will be made that the refusal to accept does not get us much further. Mr. Bridges's own answer would perhaps be Lycomedes' :

> men who would live well
> Weigh not these riddles, but unfold their life
> From day to day.

No attempt has been made in these brief notes to do more than indicate the artistic virtues and the outlook of Mr. Bridges : the elucidation is scant enough, and there was no space for reasoned criticism or for discussion of the qualities which he lacks and which other poets have possessed. But it may, in conclusion, be repeated that he is, as an artist, as careful and skilful as any poet who has ever written, and that as a man he has never lied, never posed, never assumed a factitious mood because it might impress or a factitious opinion because it might startle. He *is* sensible, and he is (in the best sense) commonplace in his outlook and in his affections and admirations ; the changing conditions of our times have affected him little ; he thinks more of the " man harrowing clods " than of the " breaking of nations " ; the river, the cornfields, the village church, the domestic fireside, do obscure for him the mental and physical struggles of our world ; he has his ideal of the sound mind in the sound body, and he cannot see why anything should modify it. But his philosophy will not stale when many of our controversialists have gone the way of Godwin and Malthus ; and a reader who went to him for knowledge of how to live would certainly not be led on the rocks, little as Mr. Bridges may directly say on the subject. Nobody could be less like an apostle, but serenity, delight, cleanliness, and honesty are in him—and courage. The thought of death does not appal him, it braces him to work and joy. " Man hath his life," says Thetis in one of his dramas, " that it must end condemns it not for naught." The same certainty is in the lyrics :

> Daily thy life shortens, the grave's dark peace
> Draweth surely nigh,
> When good-night is good-bye ;
> For the sleeping shall not cease.

> Fight, to be found fighting : not far away
> Deem, nor strange thy doom.
> Like this sorrow 'twill come,
> And the day will be to-day.

The greatest of practical truths could not be put more stoutly, nor with a finer imaginative touch.

MR. HARDY'S OLD AGE*

ONE of the last and lustiest of Mr. Hardy's poems is " An Ancient to Ancients." Another might have written it, perhaps, had another had the idea ; but no one else would have had the idea. An old man, over eighty, he talks at once to his coevals and to his juniors, an individual sympathetic to both, all too conscious of the equal fate of both, but convinced still of the necessity and the beauty of " carrying on." Of his own generation almost all have gone ; yet to them he will say :

> Sophocles, Plato, Socrates,
>   Gentlemen,
> Pythagoras, Thucydides,
> Herodotus and Homer—yea,
> Clement, Augustine, Origen,
> Burnt brightlier towards their setting day,
>   Gentlemen.

He turns at once to the opposite benches and he has a word, a bitter and a wistful word, for them also :

> And ye, red-lipped and smooth-browed, list,
>   Gentlemen ;
> Much is there waits you we have missed ;
>   Much lore we leave you worth the knowing,
> Much, much, has lain outside our ken ;
>   Nay, rush not : time serves : we are going,
>   Gentlemen.

* " Moments of Vision," 1917. " Late Lyrics and Earlier," 1922.

The latter stanza is a characteristic manifestation of
Mr. Hardy's irony ; its exaggeration, in one aspect,
is also characteristic. But it is the other stanza that
matters most, and Mr. Hardy has backed his doctrine with practice. Whatever else, in his ratio-
cination, he may have missed, he has at least preserved always his passion for life, his belief that the
game, even if it must end invariably in defeat, must
be played to the end. And it has not been merely a
theoretical conviction with him ; it has been a per-
meating faith, at once bracing his intelligence and
keeping alive his heart. In the whole records of
English literature it would be impossible to find,
not an equal, but even an arguably near competitor,
of his new book, produced by a man well over eighty.
He states that some of the verses now printed are
old ; but the dated ones are mostly very recent, and
many of those undated bear the evidence of a recent
origin—on their faces. His energy, astonishingly,
is unimpaired ; his heart remains as fresh as a boy's ;
experience has deepened his understanding, but
calloused none of his emotions ; and, most remarkable thing of all, he has continuously improved in
his art. Mr. Hardy was well advanced in middle age
when he published his first collection of poems,
though he had dallied with poetry throughout his
active life as a novelist. They were generally regarded as the interesting but crude verses of a born
writer of prose. He abandoned prose ; he has issued
volume after volume of poetry ; and the outcome
of it is that there are now many people who think
that he will chiefly survive as a great English poet
who wrote novels in his earlier years. There seems

to be some reason to suppose that such a result would not dissatisfy him. And so hale is his intelligence, so persistent his interest in his art, that, almost incredible as it might seem to one who had not read him, it would cause no surprise were he at some future date to publish the finest verses of his whole career.

Mr. Hardy's liveliness is not only evident in the poems which this substantial new volume contains ; it shows also in the preface. The preface contains some vigorous controversial remarks about certain critics who have accused him of pessimism. Men have said that Mr. Hardy looked on the darker side of life ; his answer is that he refuses to pass by facts as the Levite passed the afflicted, and that in any event " If way to the Better there be, it exacts a full look at the worst." " Should," he asks, " a shadow of such stuff as dreams are made on disregard considerations of what is customary and expected, and apply himself to the real function of poetry, the application of ideas to life ? " I imagine that nobody in his senses would wish Mr. Hardy to burke the truth as he sees it, or to suppress his honest opinions because they might offend other people's susceptibilities. Nor, indeed, if one will survey his work as a whole and not single out the expression of moods darker than usual or sentences written under the temporary influence of a rationalist logic, can one call him a denier. His deepest desires might at any time have been deduced ; in " The Oxen " and in certain passages of this new preface, they are explicit. He would like to believe. He hankers after a belief that is not his and of which he perceives the inaccessible loveliness and sweetness. On a Christmas Eve, at midnight, someone mentions the legend about the oxen kneeling in the stall, and he feels :

> If some one said on Christmas Eve,
> " Come, see the oxen kneel
>
> In the lonely barton by yonder coomb,
> Our childhood used to know,"
> I should go with him in the gloom,
> Hoping it might be so.

Some men have faith ; many, very many, live in what Dr. Johnson called "that middle state between hypocrisy and conviction " ; some find insufficient grounds for belief and hanker after it without getting it ; some, so they assure us, see no purpose in the universe, no hope of ultimate justice, no immortality in the soul, and are content to see none. Mr. Hardy was never among these last ; there are moments when he has been a transient sojourner among the first. He has been rather a passionate sceptic than a pessimist. Yet, in a less general sense, there is some excuse for those who have given him the name. He himself refers to " good Panglossians" to whom his poems may seem " to embody strange and disrespectful conceptions of this best of all possible worlds " ; I think that some who are hardly of the opinion of Dr. Pangloss might interpose that the world, however far from grace, does not deserve quite everything that Mr. Hardy has said of it. He does not slander human nature ; that never. Wherever he finds nobility, courage, tenderness, he loves them ; and they redeem the universe for him even when it looks most black. These alone make life worth living :

> I travel as a phantom now,
> For people do not wish to see
> In flesh and blood so bare a bough
> As Nature makes of me.

> And thus I visit bodiless
> Strange gloomy households often at odds,
> And wonder if man's consciousness
> Was a mistake of God's,

> And next I meet you, and I pause
> And think that if mistake it were,
> As some have said, O then it was
> One that I well can bear !

He is not a pessimist in the Swiftean sense. It is the circumstance rather than the creature that he maligns. He does, it might be urged, show a tendency to load the dice slightly in favour of malign Fate. I once heard a man say that " no husband in Hardy was ever safely dead " ; they were always liable to re-appear on the day of the second wedding. The joke was not unfair ; Mr. Hardy does incline to favour the story not of normal, but of abnormal, ill-luck ; he does show an astonishing ingenuity in construct-ing stories of misfortune, and especially of marital misfortune. There are several, startlingly summar-ised, in these volumes of poems ; as, for instance,

MR. HARDY'S OLD AGE

" A Wife Comes Back." His poems divide themselves into two classes, the narrative and the non-
narrative. The narrative poems are almost always
tragic ; and they are marred (as some of his prose
stories, including " Tess," are marred) by his determination to lay on the gloom as thick as he can. His
" Satires of Circumstance," in which a number of
preposterously grim situations and plots were compressed into a few lines each, invited and were
accorded the attention of parody, and all his books
of verse contain examples in this kind. They sometimes move even more to laughter than to tears.
Take the story that Mr. Hardy's extraordinary brain
constructed which concerns a marquis and his wife
who secured " Royal Sponsors " for their baby :

The morning came. To the park of the peer
    The royal couple bore ;
And the font was filled with the Jordan water,
And the household waited their guests before
    The carpeted door.

But when they went to the silk-lined cot
    The child was found to have died.
" What's now to be done ? We can disappoint not
The King and Queen ! " the family cried
    With eyes spread wide.

Even now they approach the chestnut-drive !
    The service must be read.
" Well, since we can't christen the child alive,
By God we shall have to christen him dead ! "
    The Marquis said.

This these extremely loyal subjects do, and the royal couple depart from " the park of the peer " without knowing what has been done ! One need scarcely bother to point out that the hopelessness of the subject has drawn Mr. Hardy into worse writing than he usually perpetrates. The first two lines are thoroughly comic. That he is preoccupied with the passage of time, with the relics of former days, with ghosts and tombstones, faded muslins and old tunes, is nothing strange ; the contemplation of transience and the regret of things gone is the mainspring of half our deepest emotions, and the source of half our poetry. Melancholy—in his poetry—is usually natural to a poet ; doubt is common ; that Mr. Hardy has been criticised in the way he suggests has been due, I think, not to his prevailing sadness or to his agnosticism, but to his habit of contemplating with too constant an eye the oddest pranks of fate.

That with all deference ; to pursue it further would be to court an error frequent in criticism of poetry : to forget the work in examination of the real or assumed doctrine. A doctrine, or conflicting doctrines, may underlie a poet's work ; a doctrine may even occasionally be formulated in it ; but no desire to argue or to disseminate a view of the universe was ever the prime motive of a poet when engaged in composition. Something, whether one of the innumerable natural images of truth, or a human relation, or an aspect of man's temporal life, or an " idea " about the universe, has aroused an emotion, and from that emotion comes a poem. Late and early his mood has habitually been melancholy ;

he has been given to regret for the past, for old happiness and old enjoyment, for one figure loved and lost, or for " the bevy now underground." Allowing his irony and his bleak fatalistic philosophy only an occasional peep in, he sits and broods in his old age over things that have gone, and draws music from that sensitive heart of his that no rationalising has ever been able to petrify. Often he is actually in a churchyard, amid the rain-worn cherubs on the tombstones, the half-effaced names, the dripping moss, the direct reminders of the dead. Wherever he starts from he reaches the same goal ; any small thing is a key which opens the chamber of his sorrows. The log slowly charring in the fire comes from the tree which he climbed and she stood under years ago ; the skeleton of a sunshade found under a cliff was left there by a woman now dead. He burns a photograph of someone, not a particular friend, and the eyes of the reproachful dead watch him from the air ; a moth beating at his window may be the forlorn spirit of the dead ; a pedigree that he is studying springs to life before him, and he meditates over all the departed generations whose blood is in his veins ; he starts out on a familiar road to pay calls, and remembers that all those he used to call on are gone. Everything is behind him and nothing before him ; he watches with resignation and melancholy the changes of his own flesh just as he watches the decay of an old ruined house where the fiddles once played and rustic feet twined in the forgotten country dances. Time after time he writes what is virtually the same poem, but the constant freshness and poignancy of the feeling

makes it always new. " The Anniversary " is characteristic :

It was at the very date to which we have come,
In the month of the matching name,
When, at a late minute, the sun had upswum,
Its couch-time at night being the same.
And the same path stretched here that people now
follow,
And the same stile crossed their way,
And beyond the same green hillock and hollow
The same horizon lay ;
And the same man passes now hereby who passed
thereby that day.

Let so much be said of the date-day's sameness,
But the tree that neighbours the track,
And stoops like a pedlar afflicted with lameness,
Had no waterlogged wound or wind-crack.
And the stones of that wall were not enshrouded
With mosses of many tones,
And the garth up afar was not overcrowded
With a multitude of white stones,
And the man's eyes then were not so sunk that you
saw the socket-bones.

It has been argued that his monotony of theme is a
weakness in him. Certainly his joys and his sunny
landscapes are almost always in the past. But he
never does anything out of mere habit, and his
genuineness and gift for characterising landscapes
and people make the one theme ever fresh. Mr.
Hardy, almost always, has written like a poet : his

work has come unpolluted from the spring, and he
has let it come as it might. And so powerful has his
emotion usually been that he has been able to write
with a rare spontaneity. He is not without art, not
without artifice ; the variety of his metres and his
stanzas is extraordinary. Yet, however complex his
form, it seems to be born with the subject ; and it is
certain that his words gush out with such power
that he can make things seem musical which no
other man dare say, and incorporate in his melodies
words which, in any other poet's verses, would sound
cacophonous. You get lines like :

> As she blent that dexterous voice
> With the ditty of her choice,
> And banished our annoys
>   Thereawhile.

or

> When moiling seems at cease
> In the vague void of night-time,
> And heaven's wide roomage stormless
> Between the dusk and light-time
> And fear at last is formless,
> We call the allurement Peace.

Had any other man written " our annoys thereawhile "
or referred to heaven's " roomage," we should have
groaned ; the force of Mr. Hardy's sincerity and
vision makes one not merely accept them, but like
them. In the second passage he is so concentrated
on his novel conception of that false tranquillity that
disguises all our mortal struggle at certain hours
that he scarcely seems to notice himself what words

he uses ; and we do not notice them either. They
are, as it were, overborne and absorbed. In a spring
poem he writes, " The primrose pants in its heed-
less rush," and the needs of rhyme lead him to
embellish a modern and simple lyric with " a maid
and her wight." Still, in many poems there is no
flaw, even on the second and more cold-blooded
reading. " The Ghost of the Past " is a poem as
musical as any that exists :

> . . . . . And then its form began to fade,
> Began to fade,
> Its gentle echoes faintlier played
> At eves upon my ear
> Than when the autumn's look embrowned
> The lonely chambers here,
> The autumn's settling shades embrowned
> Nooks that it haunted near.

Words are married to tune, communicating an exquisite tenderness.

It is the memory of that tenderness that remains
with one ; of a sensitive, generous heart which never
ceases to feel. In all Mr. Hardy's work the dominant
note is the note of Pity, not a pity born of complacent superiority, but the pity of one, fleetingly
embodied in flesh and bone, for all who sustain the
inevitable miseries of this transient life, and especially for those whom circumstances, of character or
of event, rob of what fleeting happiness they may,
as he sees it, enjoy between mystery and mystery.
In his last poem he communes with himself, ques-
tioning his motives as all honest men must question

their motives, disputing the value of his achievement as a man must do who has the sense of eternity. The last verse runs :

> " *You taught not that which you set about,*"
> Said my own voice talking to me ;
> " *That the greatest of things is charity* " . . .
> —And the sticks burnt low, and the fire went out,
> And my voice ceased talking to me.

He will find, on this score, no other accuser than himself. It is from the very depths of that compassion that the poignancy of his pessimism—if he will allow the word—springs. He stands above the world and—

> Wistful voices call
> " We are fain ! We are fain ! " from everywhere
> On Earth's bewildering ball.

Those voices are always in his ears, and their echoes are present in all his poetry. Had all of us, who call ourselves Christians, as much pity and as much love, the ball might be a little less bewildering.

MR. A. E. HOUSMAN

"A SHROPSHIRE LAD " appeared in 1896. It attracted little attention when it first came out, but it soon began to percolate underground, and after a few years it had become, what it still remains, a powerful influence over artists and the treasured companion of thousands of readers. It was a little book, and a masterpiece. Its author, when he published it, was a young man. But he relapsed into silence. He became professor of Latin at Cambridge, he edited one of the obscurest classics he could find—expending enormous labour on it and great wit—and only once or twice in twenty-six years did he publish a poem which proved that his impulses and his powers were undiminished. Now, all new (I think) except the epigram on the Expeditionary Force, forty more poems appear in a valedictory volume. Mr. Housman condescends to a short preface. It may, since it is the first statement he has ever made about his own writing, be quoted in full :

> I publish these poems, few though they are, because it is not likely that I shall ever be impelled to write much more. I can no longer expect to be revisited by the continuous excitement under which, in the early months of 1895, I wrote the greater part of my other book ; nor, indeed, could I well sustain it if it came ; and it is best that what I have written should be printed while I am here to see it through the press and control its spelling

and punctuation. About a quarter of this matter belongs to the April of the present year, but most of it to dates between 1895 and 1910.

He has waited a quarter of a century, and the spirit which prompted the delay is very evident in the preface. At all events, he has made no mistake now. If there were some who thought that any successor to the " Shropshire Lad " must be an anti-climax, they may change their minds. At first shock the reader who has cherished " A Shropshire Lad " may think, as he comes upon the familiar rhythms and thoughts, that the second book is an overflow from the first, a weaker repetition. But it will not take him long to discover that it is, in fact, a continuation, and a continuation at the old level. He will discover " The West," then " The Epithalamium," and one by one these new poems will creep into his heart and become part of him, as did the old ones. In a day he will not know from which of the two books many of these poems came.

Mr. Housman has not printed his new poems in the order of their composition, and he has given no hint as to their respective dates. It would be possible to speculate as to which were the latest written. In one or two there is a tinge of retrospect which is convincing ; and it may be that a tendency to look at things astronomically has grown on him. There are in these lyrics several audacious and magnificently successful images suggested by the contemplation of the earth as a planet—in contrast with a particular beloved spot of earth or human being. Such a phrase as :

And up from India glances
The silver sail of dawn

might have occurred in the earlier book ; but there
seems a new largeness in the picture of the dead man
who has put on his winter overcoat of land and sea,
of that other dead man (buried in South Africa) who
has the Pole Star beneath him, and of the earth's
" towering foolscap of eternal shade," circling as
the sun circles. Speculation, however, is dangerous ;
and even were full information given, " results "
would be very slight. In manner, since we know
that a quarter of these poems are new, there has been
only a slight change, if any. I should say that " Hell
Gate "—a powerful thing, which looks like the
record of a dream—was recent, but I am not sure.
It is possible that where there is a direct reminis-
cence of an early poem—as, for instance, in the line,
" The rain, it streams on stone and hillock," which
is twin of the old poem, " The wind it blows through
holt and hanger "—we are in contact with a poem
of the Shropshire Lad period. But the whole of the
new verses are so obviously by the old hand that
nothing in this way can be determined with certainty.
And the mood, whatever may be true of the manner,
has not changed at all.

It may be that, when these poems are arranged in
chronological order, those who study them will be
able to trace some slight development in Mr.
Housman's style ; but they will record no change in
his themes, none in his attitude towards the world.
All that could be said of the poet of "A Shropshire
Lad " can be said of the author of " Last Poems " :

nothing less and nothing more. He has an unquenchable desire and no hope. He is acutely sensitive both
to the cruelty and the beauty of life, but even when
most intensely aware of them he sees both under the
shadow of obliterating death and against the background of a blind featureless eternity about which he
has no theories and with which he feels not even the
slightest and most occasional mystical contact. It is
a consolation that the cruelty will pass, and a torture
that all human love and all natural loveliness must
go with the blossoms into nothingness ; he must
endure the one when he can and enjoy the other while
he may. Endurance is difficult and calls for perpetual
self-reminders, and enjoyment when keenest brings
the strongest return of the knowledge that it is transient. He is never visited by any glimmering of comfort regarding the ultimate meaning and destiny of
things ; " somehow good " has no reflection in his
vocabulary ; on the whole, should he qualify his
agnosticism in terms he would incline to the view
that the universe is under an evil government, if
any. All the old characteristic broodings recur in
the new collection. His soldiers who go doomed to
the fight are types of all mankind, battling briefly
against an invulnerable fate ; whether they are
kicking against the pricks, or stoically resigned, their
preoccupation is the same, and their end the same.
He puts it now with an ironic humour, which half
conceals pain, now simply and directly out of the
bared heart. One soldier ends his song with :

> For in the grave, they say,
> Is neither knowledge nor device
> Nor thirteen pence a day.

And another :

> So here are things to think on
> That ought to make me brave,
> As I strap on for fighting
> My sword that will not save.

He thinks as he watches another :

> Too full already is the grave
> Of fellows that were good and brave
> And died because they were.

All his doctrine about the race is summarised in two analogous passages in this book :

> Our only portion is the estate of man :
> We want the moon, but we shall get no more.

> To think that two and two are four,
> And neither five nor three,
> The heart of man has long been sore
> And long 'tis like to be.

Beyond question he states his own position in these sentences, a position put even more briefly in a couplet elsewhere :

> I, a stranger, and afraid,
> In a world I never made.

In his old book he put his conclusions in two of the finest of all his verses : the noble and massive stanzas in which he addressed his soul with " Let us endure an hour and see injustice done," and those others in which he exhorted himself, since springs must be so few, to go and look at the cherry-trees in bloom. We have them here again : " The Spartans on the sea-wet rock sat down and combed their hair " is the last line of one poem. There is another which " hath a most dying fall " and begins exquisitely, sighingly, with :

> Tell me not here, it needs not saying
> What tune the enchantress plays
> In aftermaths of soft September
> Or under blanching mays,
> For she and I were long acquainted
> And I knew all her ways.

It is spoken to all who wander with delight about the woods and fields he knew, listening as he listened to the shouts of the cuckoo, watching as he watched the falling of pine-cones and sheaves standing in moonlight, comforted as he was comforted by the Traveller's Joy that " beguiles hearts that have lost their own," and it tells them, before it is too late, to :

> Possess, as I possessed a season
> The countries I resign.

That resignation will not be completed yet ; Mr. Housman, while he is alive, will not escape himself ; he is not of those who are calloused by age. But the other resignation, after the example we have seen of his astonishing self-control as an artist, we may unhappily take to be final. He abandons his art with as beautiful a farewell as any poet ever wrote :

When lads were home from labour
  At Abdon under Clee,
A man would call his neighbour
  And both would send for me.
And where the light in lances
  Across the mead was laid,
There to the dances
  I fetched my flute and played.

The lofty shade advances,
  I fetch my flute and play :
Come, lads, and learn the dances
  And praise the tune to-day.
To-morrow, more's the pity,
  Away we both must hie,
To air the ditty
  And to earth I.

So there he leaves us : with a hundred lyrics. It is a peculiar phenomenon in the history of poetry : a hundred lyrics, of which the majority are, humanly speaking, perfect ; no failures, no padding, none of the crude attempts of youth, none of the merely habitual versifyings of senility, no effort to conquer any form but the one, none to write a " major work." No English poet has been so ruthless with himself as an artist ; that alone would make him unique. He is equally singular in manner and in attitude : a sort of blend of Baudelaire and Heine who is nevertheless as English as he could be. Posterity, which always amuses itself with this game, may " place " him. What is certain is that he is bound to be a considerable figure in our poetical history, and that his poems, unlike many great works, will continue to be widely read. It is a strange quality in him that his very pessimism attracts those who like pessimism nowhere else. He is honest and courageous ; he incites in the end, to honesty and courage ; he stimulates enjoyment even while he laments ; and his music is so beautiful that whatever he says must delight. Young men and lovers will find all their secret thoughts in him, and finding them will be comforted ; and to poets he will be a standard. Whatever his limitations may be, he has written scarcely a line which is not perfectly musical, scarcely a word which is not accurate and necessary. He has disciplined himself to such a point that there is at least one poem in his new volume which does not contain a single adjective ; he is always lucid, always truthful, and when he uses an epithet he uses it to some purpose. This is a matter apart from philosophy. Even hymn-writers could study him to advantage.

MR. YEATS'S LATER VERSE*

MR. YEATS'S "Later Poems" contains all the poems which Mr. Yeats wrote between his twenty-seventh year and 1921. The book, therefore, is a companion to the old volume of collected "Poems." It opens with "The Wind Among the Reeds " (1899), and ends with " Michael Robartes and the Dancer " (1921), spanning the distance between " The Lover Tells of the Rose in his Heart " and " A Prayer for my Daughter." Some of the finest work that Mr. Yeats has recently done has been written since the date at which this volume closes ; " All Souls' Night," for example. From any section of the book, however, very beautiful and original things might be quoted, not least among them " The Wild Swans of Coole." It begins :

> The trees are in their autumn beauty,
> The woodland paths are dry,
> Under the October twilight the water
> Mirrors a still sky ;
> Upon the running water among the stones
> Are nine and fifty swans.

He has seen them, autumn after autumn, for years ; as he watches them they rise and wheel in the sky ; he has changed, but they have not ; paddling in the water or climbing the air,

> Their hearts have not grown old ;
> Passion or conquest, wander where they will,
> Attend upon them still.

* "Later Poems," by W. B. Yeats.

There are fine passages in the series about a dying lady, a series smacking a little of the decadent 'nineties, when Mr. Yeats associated with persons with whom fundamentally he had nothing in common, but vivid, musical, full of feeling. There are many good political poems and the love poems from " Responsibilities." And there are sweet and poignant snatches such as this song from the latest book of all :

> I thought no more was needed
> Youth to prolong
> Than dumb-bell and foil
> To keep the body young.
> Oh, who could have foretold
> That the heart grows old ?

> Though I have many words
> What woman's satisfied,
> I am no longer faint
> Because at her side.
> Oh, who could have foretold
> That the heart grows old ?

> I have not lost desire,
> But the heart that I had
> I thought 'twould burn my body
> Lain in the death-bed.
> But who could have foretold
> That the heart grows old.

Many lovely things might be extracted. I think it more advisable, though, to attempt some general remarks.

The book is anything but a duplicate of its predecessor, or even a twin. Mr. Yeats's poetry is other than it was. The observation is frequently made, and it is often coupled with a suggestion that his art has deteriorated. People want him to go on writing " Innisfree." One sometimes suspects that such critics are more familiar with Mr. Yeats in anthologies than in the series of his published volumes. So far as that goes, it may be conjectured that the anthologists of the future will draw more upon this second collection than upon the first. Even omitting what are the most characteristic of his later poems, it contains several beautiful songs—the finest of all Mr. Yeats's love poems—and a noble series of political poems, plain to understand, and full of feeling. Yet much of the finest work in it is of a new kind and less obvious in its appeal. Perhaps the difference might be roughly indicated if one said that when people did not understand one of Mr. Yeats's old poems they thought it nevertheless charming, but that when they do not understand one of his new poems they think it dull. The change has happened : still, in many essentials Mr. Yeats has not changed. His preoccupation with religion remains. His attitude towards civilisation is what it has always been : and this is more important than might be thought with a man who occasionally, with Tom O'Roughley, makes remarks about logic-choppers, and says that " wisdom is a butterfly." It was in his old preface that he spoke of " a subtlety of desire, an emotion of sacrifice, a delight in order, that are perhaps Christian, and myths and images that mirror the energies of woods and streams, and of their wild creatures " ; he still, and in his poetry, stands for two cultures and two traditions, the aristocratic scholarly and the popular, both sustained by ceremony and fed by the free imagination ; he has always cared about the world and Ireland and has not changed his opinions about their diseases.

Nor has the rigour of his artistic ideals altered. Early as well as late he might have said, and with truth, that " to articulate sweet sounds together " is the most laborious and exacting trade in the world. He is the same man and the same artist ; but he has developed. He has turned his attention from one thing to another ; change has come from unchanging curiosity, certain faculties have matured and certain propensities diminished in consequence of a natural and normal passage from youth to middle age. Yet the integrity of the artist and the thinker remains unimpaired. In his writings all the important part of his spiritual and intellectual history is candidly and fascinatingly displayed and may be followed with—in both senses—admiration. A parade of " confession " he never makes, but every new discovery of knowledge, every new orientation of mind, every current of doubt and belief, hope and depression, every wavering of passion, thought, and will is, without self-consciousness, as though a man were talking in an undertone with himself, faithfully reflected. Amongst the rest we come across his thoughts about his own art. For his general speculations about art one must go to his prose works, and especially to " Per Amica Silentia Lunae." There we find him describing art as " the hollow image of fulfilled desire " ; quoting Goethe's theory, " One must

allow the images to form with all their associations
before one criticises "; declaring that " We make
out of the quarrel with others, rhetoric, but of the
quarrel with ourselves, poetry." In the poems the
more technical and personal aspects of his own work
are freely annotated. He looks back in several moods
on a time when

> I could find
> Nothing to make a song about but kings,
> Helmets, and swords, and half-forgotten things.

At one moment it seems a dim time of feeding on
memory ; at another a passing atrophy makes him
regret,

> When I was young
> I had not given a penny for a song
> Did not the poet sing it with such airs
> That one believed he had a sword upstairs

—a slightly surprising suggestion to the reader. He
fears at one moment that

> The fascination of what's difficult
> Has dried the sap out of my veins, and rent
> Spontaneous joy and natural content
> Out of my heart.

In another phase of dejection he writes :

> When have I last looked on
> The round green eyes and the long wavering bodies
> Of the dark leopards of the moon ?
> All the wild witches those most noble ladies,
> For all their broomsticks and their tears,

Their angry tears, are gone.
The holy centaurs of the hills are banished,
And I have nothing but harsh sun ;
Heroic mother moon has vanished,
And now that I have come to fifty years
I must endure the timid sun.

But in one short poem of late date he confidently
and tersely states the principal thing that has happened to his art :

> I made my song a coat
> Covered with embroideries
> Out of old mythologies
> From heel to throat ;
> But the fools caught it,
> Wore it in the world's eyes
> As though they'd wrought it.
> Song, let them take it,
> For there's more enterprise
> In walking naked.

The embroideries have gone, and, for the most part,
even the allusions to old myths. And not only in this
sense is there a new nakedness. Quite clearly Mr.
Yeats, with labour as great as ever, has been aiming
at bareness of statement, directness and economy
of language and movement springing from the commoner rhythms of speech. He never could be called
flowery ; but he had certain poetical properties,
less familiar when he began using them than when
he finished, and his earlier music, as compared with
his later, was obviously elaborate. Something has
gone, but if one magic has been lost another has

been gained ; there is a deeper if less immediately enchanting music, the starkness of the language has a charm of its own, the thought is bolder and more clear cut, the pictures more definite and only requiring attention to become invested with a glamour not ready-made. An extreme example of Mr. Yeats's later practice is the verse to a squirrel :

> Come, play with me ;
> Why should you run
> Through the shaking tree
> As though I'd a gun
> To strike you dead ?
> When all I would do
> Is to scratch your head
> And let you go.

The order is the order of conversation ; there is only one adjective and that does a great deal of work ; no assistance is invited from approved pretty words or established decorations. On occasion his later theory leads him to baldness and prosiness. He sometimes forgets that mere reminiscences are no good to the poet ; that if he must write of his memories those which will serve him are those which are vivid and certain, whenever they revive, to touch or hurt his heart. There is something a little too unbuttoned about a poem beginning :

> I remember that my grandfather O'Malley
> Used often to speak of a poor old widow
> Who had lived in a little grey cottage
> Ever since the year eighteen sixty-two
> Chiefly on beans and barley-water.

MR. YEATS'S LATER VERSE

Verse here seems an artificiality, which makes his matter less interesting than it would be in prose, particularly in prose as beautiful as his can be. This, however, is an extreme case, illustrating an interesting development. We are a long way from the kings and the stars, the roses, the pale brows and the loosened hair ; with the effort after concreteness, condensation, and a natural prose order, has come a dominating desire to tell the truth about aspects of Nature and of common experience, as well as an inclination towards close metrical discussion of intellectual problems. He has deepened, and, in the best sense, hardened. Mr. Yeats will still be found often obscure by the running reader ; but his obscurity now is never chargeable to what used to be called Celticism, to vague hinting or the auto-intoxication of a singer with a beautiful voice. Now he may be dark but is never dim. If he is hard at first sight to understand it is because he compresses overmuch, or because he gives us an allegory to which we fail to find the key, or because, with whatever exactitude, he is conducting an argument so subtle or recording a process so finely analysed that the reader who wishes to share it must make an intellectual effort on his own part.

At all events, Mr. Yeats's high rank as a poet will not be disputed by anybody who has been at the pains to become familiar with the rich and extensive body of his work. The phrase is used because a considerable demand really is made upon the reader. Mankind has commonly reserved the highest place of all for poets who, whatever else they may do for a small public with more erudition than the majority, quicker wits, subtler sensibilities, more exquisite ears, make a wide appeal by virtue of the familiarity of their themes and allusions, the directness of their emotional expression, the clarity of their language, in fact, the " commonplace " elements in them. Yet it is as absurd to ignore everyone who does not move and interest large masses of men and women as it is to run to the opposite extreme (as did certain coteries of the last century) and affect a contempt for any writer who is not incomprehensible to " the herd." It was grotesque to suppose Pater a more important man than Dickens ; but it is a mistake to despise Pater because his materials and style require a knowledge that most of Dickens's readers do not possess, and present difficulties which most of them cannot surmount. A work in Arabic would bore any one of us who did not happen to know Arabic, but it might be a great experience for a man who did know Arabic; and that is only an extreme example. I myself, when I find Mr. Yeats alluding to " the cherubim of Beaujolet " lose the point of the lines. Either I never knew what these are, or I have forgotten ; with Beaujolais I am better acquainted. To every man his interests and his medium. Even the same simple sentiment may be expressed in a vast variety of ways, even the same image in words of diverse degrees of complexity. What at one end of the scale is " I wanter giveyer the Moon " becomes, in Mr. Yeats's verse, near the other end, " Had I the heavens' embroidered cloths. . . . I would spread the cloths under your feet." And a man of analytic bent and curious in speculation will tend to find excitement in visions completely strange to most men and to present ideas

which have never crossed most men's minds. Mr.
Yeats is, of course, not always remote from the
general reader ; and a large proportion of those
poems of his which he himself would consider his
best are amongst his simplest and clearest, in conception and expression. Nevertheless, he is on the
whole to be ranked with the learned and the intellectual poets, the cryptic and the hierophantic, the
philosophers who explore strange regions of thought,
the contemplatives who burrow into the recesses of
the mind, the questioners who accept nothing which
they have not closely examined, the scholars who
make references of which the savour is reserved for
those equal in knowledge, the experimentalists who
are not satisfied with anything ready made in picture
or rhythm, the craftsmen who labour for a perfection the nature of which few will comprehend. There
is nothing in him—certainly nothing now—of the
narrow æsthete or the " superior " intellectual. But
his mind has its inclinations and his tongue its speech.
He knows where he stands :

> I know what wages beauty gives,
> How hard a life her servant lives,
> Yet praise the winters gone :
> There is not a fool can call me friend,
> And I may dine at journey's end
> With Landor and with Donne.

For another man the dream might be Chaucer and
Shakespeare, Dr. Johnson or Charles Lamb ; but
the companions of Mr. Yeats's ideal are two great
men, whose works in anything like their entirety

are unread except by a few who have found inexhaustible riches behind the classic austerity of the one and the gothic tangle of the other, deep feeling and deep wisdom in the "cold" Landor, and splendid passion, magnificent eloquence, unexcelled candour, insight, power of fine discrimination and remote analogy, in the "obscure" and "stammering" Donne. These he confesses his kindred, he pursues some of the aims of each and has rivalled some of the achievements of each. If to some extent his audience is likely to be limited like theirs he will not be surprised. It is twenty years since he said, " after all one writes poetry for a few careful readers and for a few friends," content that " if one writes well and has the patience, somebody will come from among the runners and read what one has written quickly, and go away quickly, and write out as much as he can remember in the language of the highway."

MR. EDMUND BLUNDEN*

MR. BLUNDEN was, is, and probably always will be, a poet mainly of the countryside. "Landscape poet" is a misnomer. Landscape poets are very often townsmen, with an eye for colour and shape and a feeling for nature in general, but not necessarily a knowledge of the characters or even the names of any but the commonest and most conspicuous country things, who have never shared in the occupations of a farm or the sports of a village. Lark and nightingale are well enough ; Jones's Warbler is another matter ; there is no reason to expect that poets should be expert ornithologists ; nor do they necessarily suffer by the defect. We have a very great wealth of "landscape poetry" in English, but not much has been done from the habitual countryman's angle. Mr. Blunden's work is so done. It has affinities with certain parts of Wordsworth ; but the poets nearest him are Edward Thomas, and still more John Clare, whom he has enthusiastically edited, and he often reminds us of Richard Jefferies, the essayist. The life of the country is his own life, and he finds the beautiful where a transient passenger would fail to find the picturesque. He does not, as a rule, wait for the remarkable natural conformation, or the remarkable natural effect ; and he does not usually wait for a great emotional moment in himself. But he has a steady love of the South English rural scene in all

* "The Shepherd and Other Poems of Peace and War," by Edmund Blunden. 1922. "The Waggoner," 1921.

its changes and in all its details : barns with sagging roofs, cornfields, oast-houses, clay pastures, mills, small rivers, fish pools, grass, nettles and the wild flowers of the downs. Anything in that world may give him a poem. Characteristic instances are to be found in these two extracts :

And nigh this toppling reed, still as the dead
    The great pike lies, the murderous patriarch
    Watching the waterpit sheer-shelving dark,
Where through the plash his lithe bright vassals
        thread.
The rose-fumed roach and bluish bream
And staring ruff steal up the stream
Hard by their glutted tyrant, now
Still as a sunken bough.

Up the slow stream the immemorial bream
(For when had Death dominion over them ?)
Through green pavilions of ghost leaf and stem,
A conclave of blue shadows in a dream,
Glide on ; idola that forgotten plan,
Incomparably wise, the doom of man.

These are typical lines from the many poems in which the poet muses over small slow streams full of fish—full, if one may say so, in one instance, of too many sorts of fish. This again is from " The Barn " :

    The smell of apples stored in hay
    And homely cattle-cake is there.
    Use and disuse have come to terms,

MR. EDMUND BLUNDEN

The walls are hollowed out by worms,
But men's feet keep the mid-floor bare
    And free from worse decay.

All merry noise of hens astir,
Of sparrows squabbling on the roof
Comes to the barn's broad open door ;
You hear upon the stable floor
Old hungry Dapple strike his hoof,
    And the blue fan-tail's whir.

In " Leisure " he watches dawn come over the earth
and, with delicious whimsicality, pictures " the
delighted Spirit in the dells " who

    Woos the sun's opening eye
With his droll night-whims, puffballs' pepper-gourds,
Startling white mushrooms and bronze chantarelles.

In " The Giant Puffball " one of these " drolls " is
taken singly. " Perch-fishing " has an amazingly
vivid and watery description of a catch ; " Storm
at Hoptime " describes all the movement of hopping.
A complete example is " The Poor Man's Pig " :

Already fallen plum-bloom stars the green
    And apple-boughs as knarred as old toads' backs,
Wear their small roses ere a rose is seen ;
    The building thrush watches old Job who stacks
The bright-peeled osiers on the sunny fence,
    The pent sow grunts to hear him stumping by,
And tries to push the bolt and scamper thence,
    But her ringed snout still keeps her to the sty.

Then out he lets her run ; away she snorts
In bundling gallop for the cottage door,
With hungry hubbub begging crusts and orts ;
Then like the whirlwind bumping round once more ;
Nuzzling the dog, making the pullets run,
And sulky as a child when her play's done.

This is not landscape, though there are fragments
of landscape in it ; it is a reproduction of a part of
rusticity, of rural life. Just above it is a sketch of the
village green. The yokels are playing football :

Who on the wet green whirl the ball about
With monstrous shambling kicks ; and in and out
Among them plays the mongrel black and young,
As pleased as any there, and lolls his tongue,
But near the postman, watching " how she flies,"
The older dog looks on with pitying eyes,
And thinks it only folly play, and droops
His weary head away when laughter whoops
To see tripped Longshanks floundering on his back,
With trousers daubed in mire and face all black.

Writing like this springs from daily familiarity.
But it also springs from daily delight. It is not " mere
description," as some modern writing is. Feeling is
implicit everywhere ; it is explicit in such phrases
as "sulky as a child," and " as pleased as any there ";
a pervading sentiment and awareness of the goodness of it all, a relish of the quality in everything
seen, all these perennial trifles, all these day-to-day
occurrences. These quotations are extreme examples
of reticence ; there are many poems in which the

poet makes himself much more clearly evident, and some in which the life he reflects is a background for emotions externally derived by himself or other persons. But it is almost always there. When you have read his books there have been recalled to you innumerable sounds, sights, and scents which you have experienced in the English countryside, and many which you never consciously recorded or recalled : the smells of the farmyard, the ways of poultry and cattle, the dim and stealthy movements of fish, black weeds hanging on sun-dried sluices, the texture of stone drinking-troughs, the colour of alehouse benches and the pictures on the walls, the scurryings and crawlings of insects under stones, the tone of bells, the casual encounters with wayfarers on woodland paths, the dippings of dragonflies in ponds, the aspect of a village street at noon, the writhings of worms in new-turned mole-heaps, the taste of ale under a hedge, the feel of an old dog's tongue. I huddle them together without order ; so, sometimes, does Mr. Blunden ; but he delights in them all, and he makes the reader delight too. He might say of ten thousand things what he says of the not conventionally musical practice of the woodpecker :

> From all these happy folk I find
> Life's radiance kindle in my mind,
> And even when homeward last I turn,
> How bright the hawthorn berries burn,
> How steady in the old elm still
> The great woodpecker strikes his bill ;

Whose labour oft in vain is given,
Yet never he upbraids high heaven :
Such trust is his. O I have heard
No sweeter from a singing bird
Than his tap-tapping there this day,
That said what words will never say.

The last line echoes the accents of a hundred poets ;
but Mr. Blunden differs from most of them in that
he never attempts to say this inexpressible thing.
He speculates and reasons hardly at all; his philosophy or his search for a philosophy is to be guessed ;
he does not even incite to the guessing. He is content to recount his loves and leave the argument to
someone else.

For Poetry is an expression of gratitude for things
enjoyed. The elements of Life in which the spirit
takes most intense delight and on which the memory
broods most fondly, vary from poet to poet. A man's
dominant preoccupation may be his own capacity
for action, the spectacle of other men, or of the race,
in action, the pursuit of knowledge, personal grief
and regret, the perception of the eternal behind
appearances ; there are many more. Mr. Blunden's
is rural Nature ; not Nature the personification, or
Nature the instrument of the Almighty ; the manifestations, not the power behind, though it may be
the instinctive perception of that power that gives
wonder and beauty to those manifestations. Mr.
Blunden is not entirely concentrated on this one
aspect of Life. He has written some powerful war-
poems, some exquisite love poems, a touching elegy
on a child. Yet war he sees most clearly as a cruel

disturbance of rural peace, and he is continually driven to exhibit its vileness by contrasting it with pictures of the natural beauty which it destroys and from which it drags its victims. The loves he felt (his poems are all dated) in 1914 had become intensified when he returned after his years in France, to watch the lightest gossamer and the hungriest pike with a renewed and deepened affection. A country parish will serve as a symbol for all he deals with ; and he writes of war as something inimical to the country parish. And his recollections of human relations are always thickly intertwined with wildwood flowers and mingled with the racing of mill streams and the noises of birds and beasts. There is merit in the rather Wordsworthian story of " The Silver Bird of Herndyke Mill." There are some admirably sympathetic portraits of rural characters : in " The Shepherd " for example, and in the Arcadian " Almswomen," a poem about two old women in a cottage with a flower-garden. They and their small possessions are described quietly and affectionately :

Many a time they kiss and cry, and pray
That both be summoned on the selfsame day,
And wiseman linnet tinkling in his cage
End too with them the friendship of old age,
And all together leave their treasured room
Some bell-like evening when the may's in bloom.

Yet if there be no strong force diverting him he will always return to the contemplation of country life. Not landscape in the ordinary sense. He does occasionally make a generalised picture, a few large lines

and a few selected details. But, as a rule, he does not
" compose " in that way. He sees every detail with
acute clearness, but they are all of equal importance
to him. They are important in themselves, not merely
as contributions to a picture. He loves every sound
and scent, every form of animal and plant and insect ;
each thing that lives has character to him, and he
discriminates very little between people and beasts
and flowers. They all live, ploughman and whistling
boy, heifer and fish ; they all have pleasure in their
lives, and suffer ; they all are beautiful and die.
Even timbers and stones, bells, carts, and tools seem
animated to him ; so intense is the quality of each,
so characteristic its function, so like its progress
from newness to decay to that of all things that live.

Varied as his second book is, he showed a sound
instinct when he placed at the end of it " The Last
of Autumn," a poem in which his most prevalent
mood and most habitual joy are expressed as it were
in a summary. The sun is gilding autumnal oaks.
The fields are shorn of the harvest, sheep " dapple
the broad pale green, nabbing or resting," haystacks
and hurdles gleam, and the heart, conscious of
transience,

Cannot let a bird
Chance by but counts him into memory's tribe.

He exhorts himself to note everything, however
slowly the shadows may seem to move :

Ivy with wasp and hornet buzzes still,
Blue glittering flies are sunning on the stones,
And the hives among the nettles' chalky flowers

178

Are toiling : welcome, wayside thistles' crown,
And rare-grown daisy in the meadow, shine,
Though your pale cheeks have lost their lovely red.

But the wind that frets the old and clinging leaves
Arises deep, the very dirge and knell
Of this doomed dream :
And sets the weasel, where she hangs and dries
To skin and bone, still with her whiskered snarl,
A-swaying on the barren sloe-tree's thorn. . . .

. . . .

But who may tell
When spring shall come again ? And if these eyes
Should then be shut to the brightness of her coming?
So for her phantom violets I'll not lose
These rich, these poor, these fading, glowing hills
Nor drown my joy in boding. Better it were
To be dull Thrift, than squander thus this day :
Dull Thrift, who now has sown his mite of land,
Has thrashed his corn and beans, and where the
dew's
Quicksilver bubbles lodge and shine all day
In the cabbage leaves, and the last ladybird
Beats her bright rosy way, leans reckoning coombs
And pence upon his garden palisades.

Mr. Blunden does not " drown his joy with
boding." He is one of the least sorrowful of poets ;
when he is sad there is a specific reason for it. He
communicates a steady joy, " the harvest of a quiet
eye." His work had the marks of permanence from
the start ; apart from the general merits of his early

poems, they showed an unmistakable and rare gift for the timeless phrase. " All things they have in common, being so poor," he wrote, with classic inevitability, of his two old Almswomen ; and, lying at leisure in an autumn landscape, he idly watched

The feather's fall, the doomed red leaf delaying,
And all the tiny circumstance of peace.

Those last lines, with their touch of Keats, anticipate, by the way, one of the loveliest passages in the later book, a stanza beginning :

Here joy shall muse what melancholy tells,
And melancholy smile because of joy,
Whether the poppy breathe Arabian spells,
To make them friends, or whistling gipsy-boy
Sound them a truce that nothing comes to cloy.

But the second book is very much more impressive than the first, and the third will probably be better still. A tendency to overdo dialect words and neologisms—for coining which Mr. Blunden has an extraordinary talent—has disappeared (though " slats the weazen bine " may defeat some readers) ; but he has still to make some sacrifices to euphony. Some of his lines are so crowded with consonants as to be almost unpronounceable (he lacks that strange power of Mr. Hardy's which fuses the most intractable material into music), and he still inclines to crowd his epithets and his images so that one cannot see the wood for the trees. The crowding comes from his very eagerness, the variety of his affections :

everything reminds him of something else, and everything he thinks of is a thing he has seen and noted and savoured, distinguishing its character. Nevertheless the music of the verse is growing more certain and more varied ; and the shape of the poems is better. There is still room for development, I think, in this last regard. The defects of Mr. Blunden's qualities are obvious and not easy to fight. A man whose eyes are on the near thing and not on the far horizon, will naturally be tempted to crowd his admirable details too much together ; a man so acutely sensitive to those details will sometimes dispense with a theme, and will sometimes be drawn from one to another regardless of beginning, middle, and end. One may still say of some of his poems that each line taken separately is perfect, but that the poems are not perfect. But there is no writer against whom something—usually much—cannot be said.

THE FUTURE POET AND OUR TIME

I. *The World in* 1919

HERE is our world in motion.

We see a corner of it through our eyes. A man will march down a street with a crowd, or watch the politicians' cabs turning into Palace Yard, or make speeches, or stand on the deck of a scurrying destroyer in the North Sea, or mount guard in a Mesopotamian desert. A minute section of the greater panorama passes before him.

In imagination he will, according to his information and his habit of mind, visualise what he sees as a part of what he does not see : the human conflict over five continents, climates and clothes, multitudes, passions, voices, states, soldiers, negotiations. Each newspaper that he opens swarms with a confusion of events and argument, of names familiar and unfamiliar—Wilson, Geddes, Czecho-Slovakia, Yudenitch, Shantung, and ten thousand more. For the eye there is a medley, for the ear a great din. As far as he can, busy with his daily pursuits, a man usually ignores it when it does not intrude to disturb him. When most unsettled, the life of the world is most fatiguing. The spectacle is formless and without a centre ; the characters rise and fall, conspicuous one day, forgotten the next. The newspapers mechanically repeat that we are at the greatest crisis of history, and that " a great drama is being unrolled." We are aware that the fortunes of our civilisation have been and are in the balance. But we are in the wood and cannot see it as we see the French Revolution. It is difficult, even with the strongest effort of imagination, to visualise the process as history will record it. To pick out those episodes and those persons that will haunt the imagination of posterity by their colour and force is more difficult still. An event, contemporaneously, is an event ; a man is a man who eats, drinks, wears collars, makes speeches, bandies words with others, and is photographed for the newspapers.

Yet we know that a time will come when these years will be seen in far retrospect as the years of Elizabeth or of Robespierre are now. The judgments of the political scientist and the historian will be made : these men will arrange their sequences and their scales of importance. They will deduce effects and measure out praise and blame. With them we are not concerned. But others beyond them will look at our time. We shall have left our legacy for the imagination. What will it be ? Who of contemporary figures may we guess as likely to be the heroes of plays and the subjects of poems ? Which of the multitudinous events of these years will give a stock subject to Tragedy ? Which of the men whom we praise or abuse will seem to posterity larger than human, and go with gestures across their stages, clad in an antique fashion ? For to that age we shall be strange ; whether our mechanical arts have died and left us to haunt the memory of our posterity as a race of unquiet demons, or whether " progress " along our lines shall have continued, none of our trappings will have remained the same.

But the soul of man will have remained the same.

Those elements in events and persons which fascinate and stimulate us when we are looking at our past will stir them when they brood on their past, which is our to-day. And neither contemporary reputation, nor worldly position, nor conquests in themselves, nor saintliness in itself, can secure for a man a continued life in the imagination of the race.

Contemplate our own past in the light of this conception. Who are the men of whom poets and playwrights and story-tellers have made fictions and songs ? Augustus Cæsar when he lived was the greatest man in the world : but who since Virgil has panegyrised him and who—unless some ingenious psychologist of the second-rate like Browning—would make a dramatic poem out of him ? William Wilberforce was a very good man, but his deeds and his name have survived his personality, and he will not be the hero of an epic. The Thirty Years' War was a long and very devastating war ; Gustavus and Wallenstein, in their degree, survive the purposeless series of its disasters ; and of all its events that which most vividly lives in the memory is the small thing with which it began : the flinging of two noblemen from a tower. What is it in things and men that gives them permanently the power of stirring the imagination and the curiosity of the artist ? A quality of splendour and of power that grows more certain when the dust that was its receptacle has gone to dust. The artist who shall succeed with a historical personage may make whatever implicit or even explicit commentary he likes, but in choosing his subject—or being chosen by it—moral judgment or scientific estimate will not

184

influence him. He will be the victim of an attraction beyond the will and beyond the reason. Consider who are the figures that truly, imperatively, live in the political story of the past. Not only and not all the Cæsars who fought over the known world ; not only such chivalric souls as saw, and obeyed, the visions of Domrémy, and died when the echoes of the last horn faded over Roncesvalles. The Crusades, as a whole, were a great poem, but few of the Crusaders won more than an ephemeral name in art. Cœur de Lion has been in our own time the hero of a romance, but no man is likely again to write of even a Godfrey of Boulogne. The great age of historic Greece passed and left imperishable monuments, " one nation making worth a nation's pain," but how few of her soldiers and philosophers recur to the creative imagination ! Those stories and figures from history and pre-history which do so recur are a strangely assorted collection. The Trojan War and its leading personages are a fascination and an inspiration perennially, and among those personages Helen, Hector, Achilles, Ulysses ; but not Paris or the sons of Atreus, who live but as appendages. Coldly arguing, men may ask now as they asked then, why the Greeks should take so much trouble to recover a worthless woman, why a Hector should die to keep her, why ten thousand should perish in such a cause. But to the imagination Hector, Achilles, Helen, the divine unreason of that ten years' war, make an appeal that never comes from worthier struggles and wiser people. That is true also of Antony and Cleopatra : their story to the historian and the moralist is one of ruinous folly, to the poet a

Portentous melody of what giants wasting
Near death, on what a mountainous eminence ;
Still, in the proud contempt of consequence,
The wine of life with jubilation tasting.

The figure of St. Francis has been created and
recreated in art ; like those of Nero, Philip II, and
Mary Stuart. With the mythical who are but names
we can do what we will ; Lear and Hamlet Shakespeare could cast in the sublimest mould ; with the
historical we are tied by the historical, and few are
great enough to come through the sieve. Poets have
attempted and failed to make great characters of
Becket, of Wolsey, of Strafford, and Charles I ;
their degree of failure has varied, but they have failed
as certainly as Keats would have failed with King
Stephen. The material was not there. Cromwell and
Frederick the Great at least equalled Philip II in
achievement, and excelled him in intelligence. But
Carlyle's two heroes were no true heroes for an
artist : we are too uncertain about Cromwell's inner
man, his direction ; for all his battles he could cast
no colour over his surroundings ; and as for Frederick
there was no tragedy about him—that was left for
his neighbours. A great Cromwell, in one sense,
would be an invented Cromwell ; and we cannot
invent a Cromwell because of the documents. But
Philip II, the intense, narrow, laborious, dyspeptic
bigot, sitting in a cell of his great bleak prison on the
plateau, trying to watch every corner of the world,
and contriving how to scourge most of it ; he was
contemptible, full of vices, a failure, but there was
that in him which has compelled the gaze of poets

in seclusion from the seventeenth century down to
Verhaeren and Verlaine. He had a virtue in excess.
There was a touch of sublimity about him. The
setting counts for much ; monarchs are on pinnacles.
But where is Philip IV, except for his horse-face
on the canvases of Velasquez ? Where even, as against
the man he beat, is William the Silent, who waged
a great fight against odds and died by the dagger ;
but was a cool Whig, excessive in nothing but self-
control ? He is scarcely alive ; but Satan, as Milton
saw him, reigns in hell. We must have splendour
of a sort. The normal man loves a conflagration,
though he will lend a hand in putting it out ; and if
he is putting it out the inmost heart of him will
rejoice if it be a large fire and there are very few
firemen. Vivid force, moral or non-moral, must be
there ; a Borgia, though he be as wicked as a Nero,
cannot compete with him before the imagination ;
he was commonplace and sordid and there is no
response to him.

Such passages and such people kindle us in the
records of the past. How, from this point of view,
will the last five years, crowded and full of strife,
look when we are the materials for art ?

Will the decline of Turkey command interest ?
To the historian, not to the poet, so not, ultimately,
to the generality of mankind. There is no emergence
there of the human spirit at an exalted pitch ; very
new and surprising things must come out about
Enver if he is to rank with the great adventurers of
the stage. Men may try it—they have tried most
things—but Constantinople has failed the artist
before and will again. There is something pathetic,

there might be something tragic, in the collapse of the House of Hapsburg after so many centuries, but so far as we know at present (and our statements are avowedly conjectures) there was no incident of that fall, compassed and witnessed by small intriguing men, which can redeem it from squalor and insignificance ; and not all our reiterated assurances that this is a tremendous and tragic catastrophe can invest it with the high romantic quality which comes from passion in many men or in one man, strength and a heroic struggle. The League of Nations may be the salvation of mankind, but it has come in such a way, so slowly, so reluctantly, so haphazardly, so sensibly, that (unless comedy) nothing vital will be written of its birth. Can we see a subject for a Shakespeare or a Milton in the domestic struggle here, or the fluctuations of the Balkans, or the entry of the East into the war ? These things made their differences, but will they to the artist be more than facts ? And the men. There have arisen from the populations of all countries men, many of them " great " by virtue of position, influence, achievement ; many of them disinterested and ethically admirable. The mind passes from one to another ; over some it flits, over others it hesitates and hovers. There is something of the sublime about M. Clemenceau, the old fighter, symbolising France at the last barrier : a man who, in early novels now forgotten, formulated, or refused to formulate, a philosophy of despair, and depicted a universe without principle, order, or hope, in which the stronger beast, to no end, preyed on the weaker ; a man, nevertheless, so full of vital energy, and so certain of the one thing he loved, that he desired nothing better than to continue furiously struggling under the impending cope of darkness. There are, to some of us, disagreeable things about him ; stripped of the non-essential there is something central, that is, elemental and fine. But were he of the kind that becomes legendary, should we feel that central something as still uncertain, and would it have needed a war at the age of nearly eighty to have revealed something of grandeur in him ? Is he, at bottom, clear and forcible enough ; or, alternatively, does he feel with sufficient strength, does he want anything, plan or place or spectacle, with sufficient passion ? We cannot be certain : he may be forgotten.

Something of doubt colours also one's view of America's entry and the career of President Wilson, in some regards a close analogue to that of Lincoln. The lines of that story are simple—the watching pose, the gradual approximation to war, the President's mental struggle, his decision to throw America's weight into the scale, his manifestoes to the world in the names of liberty, honesty, and kindness, his determination that the war, if possible, should be the last. But the man at the centre of this tremendous revolution of events, the mouthpiece of these great sentiments, has he that last abandonment of feeling which alone captivates the imagination of those who hold the mirror up to certain aspects of Nature ? Without denying that it may be a great blessing that he lacks that force, without presuming to know all about him that may later be revealed, I feel doubtful. Death, more particularly violent death, before the end, might have enabled artists to impute to

him something that perhaps was not there, to give
him the benefit of the doubt. But wisely or not, he
compromised at Paris. A more spontaneous man
might have ruined us all ; but if compromise is
excellent in politics, it is of small use to poets. I
doubt if the President will take his place with St.
Francis, Philip II, and Nero.

There will survive from the war, and from the
other events of our day, certain episodes which will,
as by accident, draw the notice of artists and be, as
we speak, immortalised. A few of the countless heroic
and self-sacrificing actions which men have per-
formed in every country and by every sea will be
snatched from oblivion. Tragedians, in all prob-
ability, will brood on the story of Miss Cavell. The
names of a subaltern and an airman, fortuitously
selected, will live as live those of Hervé Riel and
Pheidipiddes. But this is not what we call history.
I think that the Rupert Brooke legend will develop.
He was beautiful and a poet, and he died in arms,
young. He had wandered to the islands of the Pacific,
and his comrades buried him in an island of the
Ægean. About him they will write poems, plays even,
in which, their colour given by actions and sayings
which are recorded, he will pass through experiences
which were never his, and thoughts will be imputed
to him which possibly he never had. Two older
artists have taken a more prominent part in the war
and its politics, a part that may indisputably be called
political. Of Paderewski I know nothing, except
that a man's progress could not easily have a setting
more superficially romantic ; the strength of the
man may be guessed at by stray tokens. A person

of whom fame in art may more certainly be predicted is d'Annunzio, a man not in every way admirable, but of a demoniacal courage, who has crowned a career full of flamboyant passages with actions that, as a spectacle, are magnificent : orations pulsating with ardour for the glory and power of the Latin genius, words that were pregnant of acts, and following these, after years of reckless flying, the sudden theatrical stroke at Fiume. As a " character " he justified himself by that lawless blow ; his rhetoric finally proved itself the rhetoric of real passion, a lust for violent life, self-assertion at the risk of death, the flaunting of the Italian name ; and, felt as such, it has moved a whole army and a whole people. Whatever the results of analysis applied to his character or the ultimate outcome of his splendid *panache*, he cannot but become, to the artists of one nation at least, a hero, the material for romance.

There may be others. But, projecting myself as well as I am able, I cannot see on the larger stage, amid the great fortunes of peoples and their rulers, more than two subjects on which I think we may be positive that they will pass into the company of material to which artists return and return, subjects which already outline themselves with some clarity to the imagination and have the air of greatness.

One is the fall of the German Empire. Were it shortly to be restored, the force with which its calamities will appeal to us would be diminished : for an end must be an end. But if what seemed to happen really has happened there is a spectacle there which will appear more prodigious and more moving as time goes on—that triply-armed vainglorious king-dom pulling the world down on itself ; the long, desperate, ruthless fight against enemies ultimately superior ; the " siege " ; the quality, proud and assured if barbaric, of the Prussian spirit which filled the ruling caste and determined at once its fight and its fall. The tale is tragic, and almost epic ; the persons are not yet revealed who shall be capable of being made, on the stage or in books, the instru-ments for telling it. Certainly, though men, mis-guidedly, will attempt to make Wilhelm II sustain an artistic load to which he is not equal, the Kaiser will make no great hero or hero-villain. Possibly in some Hindenburg or other general will be found the strength, the simplicity of belief or resolve, which make a great figure ; or possibly this will be of the tragedies in which the individual humans are all pigmies subordinate to the main theme. Elsewhere, I think, is to be found a man who has about him the certain atmosphere of imaginative life. He is Vladimir Ulianoff, Lenin.

I talked a few weeks ago with a Russian in exile, a Conservative, an official of the old regime, and (I think) a Baltic Baron. He was not, therefore, sym-pathetic to the Bolsheviks or to Lenin ; he hated, though he understood, them and he loathed him. " Lenin has ruined Russia," he said, taking no pains to conceal his desire that Lenin should die. Then the imaginative man in him awoke, as it has a way of doing in intelligent Russians of all kinds, and he suddenly added vehemently : " But a hundred years hence a Hero of Legend, like Peter the Great and the Prince who first introduced Christianity into Russia."

I felt immediately that he had spoken not merely a truth, but an obvious one. Englishmen may have all sorts of opinions about Lenin ; few have heard much beyond rumour of him, but even those who are most avowedly ignorant of him or most leniently inclined to him would scarcely like to find him in their midst. Yet there is that flavour of vitality, of greatness, about him that is lacking in many who have caused misery to none and even in some of the most potent benefactors of mankind. We feel it almost unconsciously ; the recognition of it is, as it were, instinctive ; a picture of him, growing from stray scraps of news and rumour, has been forming in our minds, a picture almost from the first differentiated from that, say, of his equally active colleague, Trotsky. Trotsky, one feels, might disappear to-morrow and leave but a name and some wreckage. But the other man, if he be not in the line of Tolstoi (as some of his adherents seem to suppose him to be), is in the line of the great oriental despots, of Tamerlane and Genghiz Khan.

And we shall know more of him, far more, than we shall ever know of Tamerlane and Genghiz Khan: as much very likely as we know of Napoleon. He has no physical attributes and no material accoutrements which might lend him adventitious aid as the centre of a pageant of power, struggle, or woe : a short, bowed man in a black coat, vivacious, hedged by no formalities of ceremonial. Yet to the imagination—and it must surely be so when he is seen backward—this little fanatic, who for twenty years was hunted from exile to exile, and returned to overthrow a government and enthrone himself on the ruins of a great Empire, is the centre of Russia, seated in the middle of that enormous web of conflict and suffering like an impassive and implacable spider. We hear this and that of him. He is genial in conversation. He is not personally cruel. He is willing to slaughter thousands at a blow to realise his ideas, for he looks at human affairs historically, if with but one eye. He is a poor speaker, but his words whip audiences into enthusiasm. He thought he would be overturned in three weeks, but adapted himself with instant decision when a longer lease was offered. This man and that is jealous of him and has tried to upset him ; he has said this or that about his success and his failure ; he will fly ; or he knows he will be executed. The reports contradict each other, but the picture remains and strengthens, the picture of a man in the grip of an idea, with one of the strongest wills in the world, indifferent to the pains and pleasures of ordinary people. That ugly little face, with its swollen bald forehead, its slanting lids closing on straight penetrating eyes, its squat nose, its fleshy mouth between moustache and goatee, its smile mechanical as a mask's, will be more familiar to our descendants than to us. They will see in reverie the revolution, with vast ancient Russia as its background, and this doctrinaire tyrant as its centre, with his ragged armies, his spies and Chinamen, his motley gang of clever Jews, brigands, and mild, bearded, spectacled professors around him. They will feel his magnetism, and, whether as " hero of legend " or devil of legend, they will celebrate him.

Of these things perhaps men will write two

hundred or two thousand years hence. But the duration of human life on our planet is measured, as we
suppose, in tens of thousands of years.

We go to the grave. The sunlight comes into this
room ; it shines on the table and the books and the
papers. I listen to the twittering of the birds, shorter
lived than ourselves, and the intermittent rushing
of the wind, which, while life lasts, goes on always
the same. A car moans past ; its noise begins, swells,
and dies away. The trees wave about : a horse's
feet plod by ; the sunlight sparkles on the river and
glorifies the mud. Clouds come over. The sun, unseen, sets ; the evening grows bluer and lamps
twinkle out over the misty river. So, noiselessly,
proceeds time, and the earth revolves and revolves
through its alternations of sun and shade. These
airs, these lights and sounds, will be the same ; but
we, alive and immortal as we feel, shall have gone
and the clamour that we made will recede. To an
epoch we shall be the coloured strutters of history
and of legend ; to a later age, however remote and
whatever the accumulation of our records, we must
become august shadows like the dim kings and
fabulous empires that passed before Babylon and
Egypt. " Truly ye are the people, and wisdom shall
die with you." The sentence was written more than
two thousand years ago ; the author is unknown
and receding. Yet, obliterated in the end though all
remembrance of us may be, we shall not even on
this earth die with our bodies, and for some in-
terval, not to be computed, certain actions at this
moment in progress will endure in a sublimated
state, and certain men with whom we may even

have spoken will enlarge to a more than human stature and communicate, as they could never do in life, their essence to the enduring tradition of men. Are they those whom we have mentioned ; or are they, as they may be, others who to us are insignificant and obscured ?

THE FUTURE POET AND OUR TIME

II. D'Annunzio in 1920

A YEAR ago I made an attempt to survey the current politics of Europe not from the point of view of the statesman or of the moralist but from that of the future artist. The suggestion was made that of all the outstanding political figures of that time, though there might be many more virtuous, more disinterested, more commendable, more ultimately or immediately influential, none seemed so certain of commemoration (not necessarily complimentary) by the dramatists and poets of the future as Lenin and Gabriele d'Annunzio. The year which has elapsed, and which has ended with each of those men where he was and as conspicuous as ever, has not modified that judgment. Those two great and picturesque energies, loathed or loved but always fascinating, are still where they were. The fortress of Moscow is still unbreached and the riddle of Fiume unsolved. The precise words used here were : " A person of whom fame in art may more certainly be predicted is d'Annunzio, a man not in every way admirable, but of a demoniacal courage, who has crowned a career full of flamboyant passages with actions that, as a spectacle, are magnificent : orations pulsating with ardour for the glory and power of the Latin genius, words that were pregnant of acts, and following these, after years of reckless flying, the sudden theatrical stroke at Fiume. As a ' character ' he justified himself by that lawless

197

blow ; his rhetoric finally proved itself the rhetoric of real passion, a lust for violent life, self-assertion at the risk of death, the flaunting of the Italian name ; and, felt as such, it has moved a whole army and a whole people. Whatever the results of analysis applied to his character or the ultimate outcome of his splendid *panache*, he cannot but become, to the artists of one nation at least, a hero, the material for romance." I still believe this, but there is little consciousness of it in the newspapers.

Of Lenin we have heard much ; but the odd British indifference to d'Annunzio is just what it was. He was, in our newspapers, " Poet-Airman," then " Poet-Brigand," then " poet " or " boastful poet " or " defiant poet." But our journalists have commonly treated him as an ordinary incomprehensible foreigner. They have heard that he is a poet, but they haven't the ghost of a notion what his poetry is like. They have heard that he is an airman, but they do not attempt to imagine what his airmanship meant. They are aware that (politically) he is a nuisance, but—perhaps it is not their business—they show no signs of realising how sublime a nuisance. And their lack of curiosity is the complement of a similar lack of curiosity which has always been displayed in his regard amongst English literary people. Anatole France is, when we go further than the mere familiarity with a name, ten times better known here than Gabriele d'Annunzio. However few English people in this generation may know Italian, it is a puzzle. For it is over twenty years since the late Mr. Heinemann began publishing in this country excellent translations of d'Annunzio's plays and novels.

Their power, one would have thought, would have been recognised even by those (amongst whom I most heartily range myself) who detest the mind and morals of their author. And all the materials for d'Annunzio's public history as artist, soldier, and politician are so easily available that one would have supposed people would at least have understood how astonishing that history has been. The romantic still allow themselves to be dazzled by the characters and careers of Cæsar Borgia and Cellini. But d'Annunzio beats all the intellectual adventurers of the Renaissance on their own ground.

That d'Annunzio should not be widely popular in England is comprehensible. His novels and plays, for all their power and vividness and the goodness of the English versions, are the sort of works which make little appeal to the heart, which are deadly serious without being elevating, and which receive a second reading only from those who take a delight in his exact, rhythmical, and varied language, his eloquent discourses on the arts, and his vivid and sustained descriptions of natural beauty. His poems, which his countrymen are agreed in putting at the summit of his work, have not been (except in scraps) translated and probably could not be translated without losing much of the quality which makes them great. Nevertheless, it is very strange that there is not a more general curiosity about a man who has, as a writer, a European fame second to none, and who is unquestionably at the head of the living literature of a great European nation. We read about him in the newspapers. We joke about the problems he sets the unfortunate Powers, or we say that he is getting beyond a joke, or (if we are artists) we even secretly thrill at the sight of a man of letters beating the men of action at their own game and vying with the most daring of the young in feats of bravery. But we do not read him in England, and our critics have not for years written about him. One therefore welcomes the excellent pamphlet on him by Professor Herford* in which an attempt, however brief, is made to convey some idea of his character, of his opinions, of the scope and merit of his work, and of the latest developments of his almost incredible career. Professor Herford says that " one who is beyond all rivalry the most adored poet, in any country of our time, who has fought for Italy with tongue and pen and risked his life in her service, and whose personality might be called a brilliant impressionist sketch of the talents and failings of the Italian character, reproducing some in height-ened but veracious illuminations, others in glaring caricature or paradoxical distortion—such a man, as a national no less than as a literary force, claims and deserves close study." He might, had he chosen, have put it even more forcibly than that.

For d'Annunzio is at once a prodigy and a prob-lem ; an artistic puzzle and an extraordinary spec-tacle. He has been peculiar in every stage of his career. He was hailed as the successor of Carducci when only eighteen ; he had a world-wide fame as novelist and playwright when he was under forty ; long before the war men said that his brilliant rocket had come down, but his first careers were nothing

* "Gabriele d'Annunzio," by C. H. Herford, M.A., Litt.D. Reprinted from the Bulletin of the John Rylands Library.

like so remarkable as his latest. He has been called a
decadent and a voluptuary ; but in physical and
moral energy he is exceeded by no living man. He
has written as insinuatingly about the pleasures of
the senses as any artist in the records of literature ;
but he has never been subdued by them and has
proved his ability to lead a life of iron austerity.
Critics, ten years ago, talked of him as a man whose
powers were spent, whose best work was done, and
who was now conspicuous only as a dandiacal and
extravagant *poseur* with a passion for self-advertise-
ment and a surpassing idea of his own importance ;
no story that was ever told of him was to his credit ;
and everything about him, including his physical
appearance, was the subject of unfavourable comment. But the artist had a new birth ; the ageing
dandy put on a uniform ; the *poseur* showed a contempt for death, and the voluble boaster a capacity
for firm and instant action. The gilded young artist,
to whose pleasure and fame all the world and all
history must minister, is now the bald and bullet-
marked veteran who sits on his little Dalmatian
platform for the sake of a national idea and coolly
defies the embattled navies of Europe and America
to touch him. Reading his books, one does feel an
inexhaustible energy, but one can only with great
difficulty believe that story.

Such a conglomerate cannot be analysed or explained in a few pages : it may briefly be illustrated by a few references. His poems of forty years
ago were the poems of a young erotic, bathing in
sensuality—a sensuality, be it understood, not
entirely or mainly sexual, but so luxurious and so

egotistic that nothing but a gradual complete surrender to the senses could have been expected. There
was a toughness behind ; had there not been he
would have ended as the common decadent ends ;
but in what a strange conjunction his strength was
found ! Listen to Professor Herford on the novels
which succeeded those early poems :

> D'Annunzio's sensuality asserts itself still, as
> always ; but it appears here as a Rubens-like joy
> in intense impressions ; now a copper-coloured
> storm sky, now a splash of blood, betrays his
> passion for the crude effects of flame and scarlet,
> most often where they signify death or ruin. He
> imagines voluptuously as always, but his volup-
> tuousness here feeds not in the lust of the flesh,
> but in the lust of wounds and death. When he
> describes the fighting in the church, he spares
> you as little as Homer ; you are not told merely
> that a man was stabbed, you are made to see the
> blade shear away the flesh from the bone.

The names of how many perversions will rise to the
tongue of the pathologist who reads that passage !
What biographies we are accustomed to associate
with men of whose work such things can usually be
written, what lost self-controls, what consumptions,
what lunacies ! Or take the next novels, "The Child of
Pleasure " and " The Victim," with their virtuosity,
their heroes almost reminiscent of Des Esseintes,
connoisseurs in metals, ivories and stuffs, marbles
and myths, wines, landscapes and mistresses, books
in which the tenderest feelings of humanity appear

only to be tasted like the material things, books at once cruel and enervating. The creative energy was there, but who could have expected an imagination to have rioted in such excesses without becoming demoralised, or an energy to persist which was directed to such ends? "The Triumph of Death " followed—a symphony of melancholy and cruel strains, full of magnificent lamentations and ending in a double suicide; "The Dead City "—a most powerful work, but sultry, stifling, deliberately morbid and, in its conclusion, wantonly brutal; "The Virgins of the Rocks "—one of the most exquisitely written of prose fictions, but leaving the reader drained and sapped as after a day of rich lamenting music too prolonged. The three women, beautiful and ineffective, superb, and sterile stand hopelessly in the darkened and crumbling rooms, on the still sunbaked terraces, or in the garden where the old fountain plashes its monotonous tune. The young man contemplates them one by one, and behind his fastidiousness and his sumptuous dreams lies a perfect despair. Any page might be quoted. Here is the end :

Anatolia had sat down beside her pensive brother ; she had thrown one arm round his neck, and her brow seemed gradually to clear as if some inner light were rising. Massimilla seemed to be listening to the faint, unquenchable voice of the spring ; sitting with the fingers of her hands clasped together, holding within them the weary knee.

Over our heads the sky bore no traces of clouds,

save a slight shadow like the ashes of a burnt-out
funereal pyre. The sun was scorching the peaks
all around, outlining their solemn features on the
blue sky. A great sadness and a great sweetness
fell from above into the lonely circle, like a magic
draught into a rough goblet.

There the three sisters rested, there I caught
their final harmony.

" Here," concludes the page, " endeth the book of
the virgins and beginneth the book of grace." It is
all very beautiful—as beautiful in places as Chopin,
in others as Giorgione ; it is full of perfect pictorial
compositions, and there is an unusual gentleness in
it. But it is not the sort of thing that is commonly
written by the President of a Republic, much less
by a freebooter. But twenty years ago d'Annunzio
discovered his politics. The sensuality, the riot of
language remained, but a new purpose crept in,
expressed originally in the crudely Imperialistic
way that one would expect from a patriot who was
a confessed admirer of Nietzsche. The year of " Il
Fuoco "—Anglicè, " The Flame of Life "—the novel
of Venice in autumn, gorgeous in colouring and repulsive in story—was the year of d'Annunzio's
foreign tour, which determined his mission of re-
calling Italy to her past Imperial glories ; and until
the war the old strains mingled with the new. At
fifty-two he was making in Rome, to a huge multitude, a speech which is said to have hastened Italy's
entry into the war. He put on a uniform, took to the
air, was decorated, and was wounded. At fifty-six
he had made his famous flight over Vienna, and Mr.

James Bone could write of him, who had passed through so much of Wagner and Zola, Nietzsche and Huysmans and Maeterlinck, in these terms :

> Conversation died instantly as an airman, very different from the others, came hurrying towards us—a rather small, very quick, clean-cut figure, wearing large smoked glasses and white gloves with the wrists turned down. . . . The nose was rather prominent, complexion not dark but marked a little, the whole profile very clear, making one think not of a Renaissance Italian, but of a type more antique, an impression accentuated by his rather large, beautifully-shaped ear, very close to the head. The body denied the age that was told in the face, for all its firmness. One's first impression was of a personality of extraordinary swiftness and spirit still at full pressure, remorselessly pursuing its course " in hours of insight willed." . . . The whole surface of d'Annunzio's personality suggested a rich, hard fineness, like those unpolished marbles in old Italian churches that gleam delicately near the base where the worshippers have touched them, but above rise cold and white as from the matrix. . . . There was something of the man of fashion in the way he wore his gloves, and in his gestures, but nothing one could see of the national idol aware of itself.

But Nietzsche at that age had died, an invalid, in a madhouse.

Accident, if you can call it accident, has favoured d'Annunzio. The whole world has been annoyed by his exploits at Fiume, but the whole world has been unable to turn him out. One party cannot attempt to evict him for fear of incensing the Italian nation ; another is impotent because of the risk to the loyalty of the Italian army. There he sits : a man of nearly sixty who, until six years ago, was regarded as a flamboyant pretender with great rhetorical gifts, a dilettante with hypertrophied senses ; a man of bold words suffering from the usual disabilities of the voluble and the picturesque. After all his talk about splendour and luxury, painted palaces and sobbing fountains and languishing Madonnas, all his easy contemptuousness and pride, inhalations of incense and rollings of cigarette papers, he is installed in the barrack at Fiume, Chief of State and head of his Army. The accounts of his daily life there given recently by a *Times* correspondent who had visited the port were almost too impressive to be comic. His navy—a Dreadnought, some cruisers, some torpedo-boats—lies on the water under his windows, spick and span and ready for action. His Army—a few thousands of enthusiastic youths—is so devoted to him and the cause that it rehearses by advancing over open ground with live bombs, a rain of machine-gun bullets twelve inches above its head : the day's result being often a dozen casualties. This may not be war, but it is, in a manner, magnificent. The poet rises early ; studies plans of defence at his headquarters ; confers with his own commanders or (on occasion) with the Italian commanders ; arranges mysteriously for the maintenance of his forces and the civil population ; and makes continual speeches which are said, for sheer mass of music and luxuriance of image, to excel anything he has ever done. In the intervals of his daily routine he still, apparently, writes ; and he has found time to construct for his little Sparta a constitution embodying all the latest known democratic devices from Nevada and Oregon. His power, we are always told, is waning. But he has not resigned yet ; and we had heard those stories for months when, during a panicky period in Italy, our newspapers suddenly began speculating as to whether he might not march on Rome and even make a bid for the throne. One had a sudden vision of a descent on Venetia with a few thousands—a progress during which half the youth in the Italian Army might flock to his banners—an entry into the capital, a triumphant speech, a brief dictatorship and a collapse. It was only a dream—a dream of confusion and destruction which one watched as one watches a fire or a devastating storm, or any other splendid and undesirable thing. Probably there was never any chance of it. Very likely d'Annunzio himself, who seems to have shed his cruder Nietzschianism and to have elements of cool if audacious statesmanship in him, is not inclined to precipitate ruin for the sake of a display, and has no illusions as to the possibility of a permanent success. But the mere fact that other people should have been tempted to play with the idea shows the impression that they have subconsciously received from him. They have realised that he is fearless, energetic, and ruthless beyond the normal of mankind. They feel in d'Annunzio— what Renan saw in Napoleon, who was a less complete example—a reversion to the old *condottiere* type. He has baffled everybody by sticking at nothing ; and, unlike most men who stick at nothing, he is utterly indifferent to the safety of his own skin. He would be a remarkable phenomenon in contemporary Europe even were he a mere professional soldier of fortune or a common political bandit. His aspect would still, like that of the tiger, attract by its qualities of strength and ferocious grace. Had he been no more than an adventurous Italian captain his little Adriatic romance might have secured him the attention of the descriptive historians of the future and dramatists in search of a fiery subject and a picturesque setting. But these exploits in war and politics, coming at the close—or, as it may be, in the middle—of so eminent and prolific an artistic career as his, make him unique. In his surging and sumptuous Venetian book the hero made a tremendous speech on " the dreams of domination, of pleasure, and of glory that Venice has first nursed and then suffocated in her marble arms " ; and the author, analysing the effects upon the hearers of that panegyric of beauty and power, said that " some one among them already imagined himself crumpling laurel leaves to perfume his fingers, and some already dreamt of discovering at the bottom of a silent canal the ancient sword and the old, lost diadem." D'Annunzio was already among the last, but for most dreamers it is one thing to dream and another to act. He attracts with the triple force of character, of genius, and of idea ; and no stage manager could have provided him with a more dazzling series of backgrounds. This is not the place in which to discuss the wisdom or folly of his recent acts and the justice of his political aims. As for the man himself, I can only say that I heartily sympathise with Henry James, who compared his search for d'Annunzio's radical defect to that of the plumber who, with his little lamp, scours a house in the endeavour to locate a mysterious bad smell. His plans may end in smoke ; his art may be defective ; we may dislike his character and even regret his survival, but it is impossible wholly to laugh at him or to deny him admiration ; and we may conjecture that his biography a hundred years hence will be regarded as one of the most astonishing and engrossing chapters in the history of literature.

PROSE AND MORTALITY

IN recent years several editors have put together anthologies of English prose passages, among them Mr. S. L. Edwards (" An Anthology of English Prose ; Dent), Messrs. Broadus and Gordon (" English Prose " ; Milford), Mr. Treble (" English Prose " ; Milford), and Professor Cowl (" An Anthology of Imaginative Prose "; Simpkin). Only the last of these books has much in common with the " treasury "* now presented by Mr. Logan Pearsall Smith. There are many kinds of good prose, of which Samuel Butler's is one, Jane Austen's another, Cowley's another : but the last two of these authors do not appear, and the first is only here by favour. A few exceptions are made, presumably owing to personal predilections or a feeling that such and such a great prose name should not be omitted. Swift is an instance. His prose, the faithful reflection of his mind, has many qualities, but it is out of place here. Generally speaking, to satisfy Mr. Pearsall Smith, in his present capacity, it is not enough—in fact, it is not anything—that prose should be adequate to its purpose, neat, easy, vivacious, well-knit. It must be prose on what by common consent is the highest level of prose, prose impeccably written, and prose with a dignity, a richness, a sonority or a sweetness of flow that rival the attributes of great poetry. Almost all his examples come into this category : he has no room here for the most vigorous pages of

* " A Treasury of English Prose." Edited by Logan Pearsall Smith. Constable.

Scott or the most amusing chapters of Dickens. His extracts are to be detachable jewels, gorgeous or exquisite. On his fly-leaf he quotes Keats :

> I had an idea that a Man might pass a very pleasant life in this manner—let him on a certain day read a certain page of full Poesy or distilled Prose, and let him wander with it, and muse upon it, and reflect from it, and bring home to it, and prophesy upon it, and dream upon it : until it becomes stale—But when will it do so ? Never— When Man has arrived at a certain ripeness in intellect any one grand and spiritual passage serves him as a starting-post towards all the two-and-thirty Palaces. How happy is such a voyage of conception, what delicious diligent indolence !

" Distilled Prose," " grand and spiritual passage " : the editor gives no other explanation than this second-hand one, but that is enough.

We must grant Mr. Pearsall Smith his ground, but on that ground every reader is sure—as an anthologist's readers always will be—occasionally to quarrel with him. His earlier selections, from the Bible, Donne, and Jeremy Taylor, could not, I think, have been better. He was bound to fill a good deal of his space with the seventeenth-century religious writers. He does not overlook South ; and he gives a numerous and glittering selection from Milton, one of the few English writers who have contrived to keep their singing-robes about them, with whatever effort, when writing about every sort of mundane subject. He has found almost everything

211

that he could have wanted in the writers of the eighteenth century, and he gives many perfect passages
from Coleridge, Shelley, Keats, and Landor. But to
some of the Victorian writers, and to some of our
contemporaries (though he has quarried some exquisite things from unlikely places) he does, if he
will allow me to say so, less than justice. We could
have spared some of the eleven pages of Emerson
for the sake of some of the best paragraphs of Ruskin,
who is given only two pages. The single extract
from Cardinal Newman (whose " Idea of a University " should have been searched) does not represent
him, and no single extract could. There are two—
there might well have been more—extracts from
Mr. Doughty's " Wanderings in Arabia."   The
passage from Samuel Butler is more sustained than
Butler's wont, but scarcely worthy of inclusion,
though the reader would appreciate in any surroundings his last sentence, " I am not very fond of Milton,
but I admit that he does at times put me in mind
of Fleet Street." Mr. Shaw appears and Henry
James ; there are good extracts from Mr. Santayana
and Mr. Lowes Dickinson. But Mr. Conrad's works
—both his Reminiscences and his novels—should
have yielded many more than two pieces, and some
admirable modern writers of coloured, musical, and
affecting prose are omitted altogether. Mr. Hardy
is a curious omission. Mr. Chesterton, as a rule,
troubles too little to be a good subject for this anthologist ; the journalist and the tumbler are always
breaking in ; the poet appears arm-in-arm with the
politician, an exasperating contiguity. But I think
that exploration would have been rewarded even

had our collector gone no farther than the splendid
last pages of " The Short History of England."
From Mr. Hudson's books, especially from " A
Crystal Age " and " Far Away and Long Ago,"
passages, I think, could have been taken which would
have competed respectably with many that are here;
Mrs. Meynell's essays and Mr. Bertrand Russell's
last book should be drawn on ; and where is Mr.
Belloc ? Rupert Brooke said that Mr. Belloc had a
better prose style than any man alive. I should not
dispute that : it is a clear, a precise, an economical
style that serves admirably all the diverse uses to
which its owner puts it. And it often rises, always
quietly, where some poignant thing is clearly seen,
into sentences of noble beauty. These are liable to
occur almost anywhere ; for instance, in a digres-
sion during an article on strategy. Possibly because
he began his career with public facetiousness about
" purple patches " he often seems to allow a promis-
ing passage to break its back because he will not
seem artificial or affected. He fetters his consciously-
exercised powers and he can seldom let himself go,
as it were, unconsciously. In his books it would therefore be far more easy to find short passages than
long ones of the kind included in this anthology ;
for any other sort of prose anthology his work should
be thoroughly ransacked. Nevertheless there are
long ones. There are certainly several in " The Four
Men " and in the book of essays. There is a long
passage in " The Absence of the Past " which begins :

There was a woman of charming vivacity,
whose eyes were ever ready for laughter, and

whose tone of address of itself provoked the
noblest of replies. Many loved her ; all admired.
She passed (I will suppose) by this street or by
that ; she sat at table in such and such a house ;
Gainsborough painted her ; and all that time ago
there were men who had the luck to meet her and
to answer her laughter with their own. And the
house where she moved is there, and the street
in which she walked, and the very furniture she
used and touched with her hands you may touch
with your hands. You shall come into the rooms
she inhabited, and there you shall see her portrait,
all light and movement and grace and beatitude.

But it is a stupid thing to spend much time talking
about the omissions from a good book ; only less
so than it would be to complain that it is one sort of
book and not another sort. Mr. Pearsall Smith set
out to collect prose passages of a certain, the most
poetical and resounding, kind ; and he has made
an admirable and a learned choice. A perusal of his
specimens confirms in me an opinion previously
formed as to the nature of this kind of prose in
English. It is that we have a canonical style for such
prose, and that such prose most frequently arises
from meditation on a definable kind of subject.

In great writers and small, in those whose prose
marches always with majesty and in those with
whom eloquence is infrequent, in the graceful and
the ungainly, in the magisterial and the familiar,
this thing is to be discerned : that their prose is
least personal when at its highest flights. The observation is common that we have in England no

standard and accepted prose style, but a medley of manners which are continually increasing in number. This is true. But it has not been generally noticed that amongst those passages of English prose, drawn from authors of all our literary ages, which are received as being the most sublime and the most musical—passages which have been, and must be, the first resort of all anthologists of our prose who are in search of those attributes of power and beauty —there is a strong likeness of form and feature. There is more : the resemblance is often so close that the differences, normally marked, between the styles of writers divided by a great gulf of time are in such sentences not to be distinguished. Styles so various on the lower plane meet, as it were, on the higher : there is an established, an inevitable, manner into which an Englishman will rise when his ideas and images lift into grandeur. It is the style of the Authorised Version, a style in process of formation long before the date of that Parthenon of our prose, but reaching in that its perfection, and by means of that made an element of the air which we breathe, and many generations before us have breathed, in childhood. Even in writers who never entirely lose the marks of their eccentricity the most eloquent " purple patches " are always reminiscent. Emotion deepens suddenly, or reaches an expected climax ; the results of reflection are summarised ; by whatever route, the author comes to a place at which his expression assumes a sublimity of imagery and a perfection of rhythm ; and with the emotion he communicates is always mingled the throe of recognition. The note has been struck and a hundred neighbouring strings respond. The writer has stepped off the common road and into that chapel where there is one ritual and one mode of incantation. " Man that is born of a woman, hath but a short time to live, and is full of misery. He cometh up, and is cut down like a flower ; he fleeth as it were a shadow, and never continueth in one stay." It is the Prayer-Book of 1549. " Thou hast drawn together all the far-stretched greatness, all the pride, cruelty, and ambition of man, and covered it all over with these two narrow words, *Hic jacit*." It is Sir Walter Raleigh. " These wait upon the shore of death, and waft unto him to draw near, wishing above all others to see his star that they might be led to his place ; wooing the remorseless Sisters to wind down the watch of their life, and to break them off before the hour." It is Bacon. " A memory of yesterday's pleasures, a fear of to-morrow's dangers, a straw under my knee, a noise in mine ear, a light in mine eye, an anything, a nothing, a fancy, a chimera in my brain, troubles me in my prayer." It is John Donne. " Methusalem, with all his hundreds of years, was but a mushroom of a night's growth to this day ; and all the four Monarchies, with all their thousands of years, and all the powerful Kings, and all the beautiful Queens of this world, were but as a bed of flowers, some gathered at six, some at seven, some at eight—all in one morning in respect of this day." That too is Donne, and his subject Eternity. " Since the brother of Death daily haunts us with dying Mementoes, and Time that grows old itself bids us hope no long duration, diuturnity is a dream and folly of expectation." That is Sir Thomas Browne. " They that three thousand years agone died unwillingly, and stopped death two days, or stayed it a week, what is their gain ? Where is that week ? " That is Jeremy Taylor. " When all is done, human life is, at the greatest and the best, but like a froward child, that must be played with and humoured a little to keep it quiet, till it falls asleep, and then the care is over." That is Sir William Temple. " The present is a fleeting moment, the past is no more ; and our prospect of futurity is dark and doubtful." That is Gibbon. " The stars that still sojourn, yet still move onward ; and everywhere the blue sky belongs to them, and is their appointed rest and their native country and their natural homes, which they enter unannounced, as lords that are certainly expected, and yet there is a silent joy at their arrival." The argument to the " Ancient Mariner " needs no specification. " Laodameia died ; Helen died ; Leda, the beloved of Jupiter, went before. It is better to repose in the earth betimes than to sit up late ; better, than to cling pertinaciously to what we feel crumbling under us, and to protract an inevitable fall." That is from a dialogue of Landor's. " And it would not taste of death, by reason of its adoption into immortal palaces; but it was to know weakness, and reliance, and the shadow of human imbecility ; and it went with a lame gait ; but in its goings it exceeded all mortal children in grace and swiftness." That is Charles Lamb. " In her sight there was Elysium ; her smile was heaven ; her voice was enchantment ; the air of love waved round her, breathing balm into my heart : for a little while I had sat with the gods at

their golden tables, I had tasted of all earth's bliss."
They have quoted that passage from Hazlitt's " Liber
Amoris " a thousand times. " Like God, whose
servants they are, they utter their pleasure not by
sounds that perish, or by words that go astray, but
by signs in heaven, by changes on earth, by pulses
in secret rivers, heraldries painted on darkness, and
hieroglyphics written on the tablets of the brain."
That is de Quincey. " And again the sun blinks out,
and the poor sower is casting his grain into the
furrow, hopeful he that the Zodiacs and far Heavenly
Horologes have not faltered ; that there will be yet
another summer added for us and another harvest."
That is Carlyle. " To what port are we bound ? Who
knows ? There is no one to tell us but such poor
weather tossed mariners as ourselves, whom we
speak as we pass, or who have hoisted some signal,
or floated to us some letter in a bottle from far." It
is from Emerson. " Not to discriminate every moment
some passionate attitude in those about us, and in
the brilliancy of their gifts some tragic dividing of
forces on their ways, is, on this short day of frost
and sun, to sleep before evening." That, if modern
in conception, altogether traditional in cadence and
in the phrasing of its close, is from Pater's " Renaissance." " We can therefore be happy in our sorrows,
happy even in the death of our beloved who fall in
the fight ; for they die nobly, as heroes and saints
die, with hearts and hands unstained by hatred and
wrong." A peroration : the peroration from the Poet
Laureate's " Spirit of Man." " And in the autumn
before the snows come they have all gone—of all
that incalculable abundance of life, of all that hope

and adventure, excitement and deliciousness there is scarcely more to be found than a soiled twig, a dirty seed, a dead leaf, black mould or a rotting feather." Mr. H. G. Wells, never a careful artist or fully aware of what language can be, permits himself some looseness in the phraseology of the passage from which that sentence comes, but he too falls, as it were unwittingly, into the old music. And here, from another living author,is a piece of declamation which contains, indeed, sentiments and words which would have been foreign to the seventeenth century, but is a true child of its loins :

We survey the past, and see that its history is of blood and tears, of helpless blundering, of wild revolt, of stupid acquiescence, of empty aspirations. We sound the future, and learn that after a period, long compared with the individual life, but short indeed compared with the divisions of time open to our investigation, the energies of our system will decay, the glory of the sun will be dimmed, and the earth, tideless and inert, will no longer tolerate the race which has for a moment disturbed its solitude. Man will go down into the pit, and all his thoughts will perish. The uneasy consciousness, which in this obscure corner has for a brief space broken the contented silence of the universe, will be at rest. Matter will know itself no longer. " Imperishable monuments " and " immortal deeds," death itself, and love stronger than death, will be as though they had never been. Nor will anything that *is* be better or be worse for all that the labour, genius, devotion, and suffering of man have striven through countless generations to effect.

This passage, summarising the conclusions that natural science unaided has been able to reach, is detached from a longer one : it occurs in Lord Balfour's " The Foundations of Belief."

There is one music and one speech in all these extracts. It is not the result of deliberation, but it is not an accident, that they have so much else in common, that their very subjects are analogous. Chosen, however genuinely, at random and without afterthought, if they are chosen from the best, they will be variations on but a few related themes and half of them will be inspired by the direct contemplation of death. There are innumerable subjects which engage the attention, and they may be seen in countless aspects ; but that large utterance comes chiefly to English lips when things, of whatever nature they may be, are regarded *sub specie æternitatis*. Whatever a man's philosophy and whatever his mood, when he speaks with this music, he speaks with the voice of mankind, awed and saddened by its inscrutable destiny. Time, Death, Eternity, Mutability : those words, the most awful that we know, insistently recur. It is they, unuttered yet present, which give their grandeur to pronouncements of many kinds which do not relate directly to the general operations of Time or of Death : to Burke's passage on Marie Antoinette, to Johnson's Preface to his Dictionary, to Gibbon's moonlight reverie on the conclusion of his History. Those names, those figures with their skirts of thunder and doom, trail through all our literature with a majesty that no others possess. Apostrophising those our shadowy tyrants, celebrating them, rebelling against them, we may clothe our conceptions in many images, though even here, for the most part, we must observe a tendency, natural and spontaneous, to choose as tokens and ornaments a few, in the earthly sense, universal and perennial things. But those shapes tower over our whole world. Anything we look at in the sunlight, a wave, a weed, a travelling insect, may be like a window opening out to them ; and at night, under the dark sky, so actual and so symbolical, the reflective man is always aware of them. We have our activities and our distractions. We must satisfy our carnal cravings, eat, drink, and sleep ; between birth and death, under that immense and unresponsive heaven, we build and dig, hunt and dance, carve and paint, intrigue, copulate and kill. But whenever the moment comes that we turn round from our toys it is one spectacle that we see : life proceeding from darkness to darkness, change, dissolution, and death. And the greatest utterance of our tongue is a chronicle, again and again resumed and repeated, of the wonder and dread, the certain regret and the wavering hope which that spectacle arouses in hearts which have immortal longings but have loved transient things : a chronicle of grass that withers, and of leaves that fall, of girls like flowers who fade like flowers, of conquerors who are dust, blown about, of tough oaks that decay, of stone temples and pyramids that as surely, after a few more years, fall into dust, of the world's past, and the past of the individual which cannot be

recovered, the innocence and the illusions of childhood, the loss of which typifies all loss and their
beauty that Eden to which, with the shadow approaching, we pitifully aspire : all framed by the
most abiding things that our senses know, the sea
and the wind and the hills, the seasons which come
for all generations in their order, the stars, constant,
silent, vigilant over all : those also transitory after
their own kind, arching to their fall in epochs beyond our computation or guessing, but in relation
to us steadfast and immutable.

They say (though I do not believe it) that an age,
even if it be still far distant, is coming in which the
present preoccupations of man, both physical and
mental, will have vanished and new passions and
new hopes will have taken their place. Our contact
with each other is as yet imperfect ; psychological
discovery is only beginning ; the gates between
mind and mind will all be broken down ; it will not
be a question of universal candour but of automatic
communication and sympathy. The individual will
be identified with the race, will live only in the life
of the race, will not merely not fear but will not even
think about any death which does not involve the
death of the race. The race will be one animal ; its
members, sloughed and replaced, will want no more
immortality than that qualified perpetuation which
the race can give ; no two persons will be more to
each other than any other two ; Man will really be
Man and will cease to be men. Should that time come
(which, speaking diffidently, it will not) the voice
of Man may change. His most eloquent words may
be other than they are now, and even though, in his

corporate form, he is still more deeply stirred by frustrations that we cannot conjecture, the range of his imagery will have altered, he will have new symbols for his regrets, and new comparisons for his ideas. Pending that change there is no reason to suppose that the essential, or to a large extent the incidental, material of our poetry, or of such of our prose as aspires to the condition of poetry, will substantially alter. We speak most sublimely of what moves us most deeply.

But this is not to say that we should wish that such speech, at the cost of such experience, should be more than intermittent. Sun, sheep, and children may take a sober colouring from the eye that has been much busied with such watchings, but they were not put there solely for that purpose ; even if we profess ignorance of the reasons for their existence, we shall employ ourselves better if we act on the assumption that they were not. The last word, after so prolonged a meditation on the incomprehensible, may lie with Stevenson, who, not unaccustomed to the thought of death and not incapable of poetry, wrote an essay on the subject which might not supply passages " distilled " enough for this book, but contains many so sensible that they might well be reprinted in others. " The changes wrought by death," he said, " are in themselves so sharp and final, and so terrible and melancholy in their consequences, that the thing stands alone in man's experience, and has no parallel upon earth." That opening might have led to a piece of great orchestral prose ; but he turned on himself and wrote instead some pages of cheerful colloquial prose, sprinkled with fine sentences. In all views and situations " there is but one conclusion possible : that a man should stop his ears against paralysing terror, and run the race that is set before him with a single mind " ; and " as a matter of fact, although few things are spoken of with more fearful whisperings than this prospect of death, few have less influence on conduct under healthy circumstances." But notice, even in this essay, the old lift, the old attitude, the old accents, when momentarily he looks out over the other wall : " Into what great waters, not to be crossed by any swimmer, God's pale Prætorian throws us over in the end ! "

INDEX

AKENSIDE, Mark, 57. 60
" Amelia," 57
Arnold, Matthew, 2, 65-66
78-79, 88-97; "The Scholar
Gipsy," 6 ; " Essay on Jou-
bert " quoted, 65
Austen, Jane, 78 ; her prose,
210

BACON, 111-112, 216 ;
" The Advancement of
Learning " quoted, 119
Bagehot, Walter, 70
Balfour, Lord, quoted, 219-
220
Barbauld, Mrs., 60
Baudelaire, 158
Beeching, Canon, 26
Belloc, Hilaire, 213 ; " The
Absence of the Past "
quoted, 213
Bewsher, Paul, " Nox Mor-
tis," 31
Blair, Robert, 60
Blake, William, 55
Blunden, Edmund, 128, 171-
182
Bone, James, on D'Annunzio,
205
Bottomley, Gordon, quoted,
46
Bradlaugh, Charles, 89
Bridges, Robert, 83, 109,
122-140 ; quoted, 27 ;
" The Spirit of Man "
quoted, 218
Brontës, Alice Meynell on
the, 114
Brooke, Rupert, 38, 190 ;
quoted, 39, 213
Browne, Sir Thomas, quoted,
216
Browning, Robert, 57, 184 ;
quoted, 26
Bruce, James, 61
Burke, Edmund, 57, 70, 220

Burns, Robert, 80
Butler, Samuel, 210 ; quoted,
212
Byron, John, 61
Byron, Lord, 48

CAMPBELL, Thomas, 48
Carlyle, Thomas, 63, 186 ;
quoted, 18, 218
Cavell, Miss Edith, 190
Cellini, Benvenuto, 199
Chaucer, 56, 169
Chesterton, G. K., 2, 212 ;
the " Victorian Com-
promise," 52
" Choice, The," 50
Chopin, 204
Churchill, Charles, 57
Churchill, Winston, 70
Clare, John, 128, 171
Clemenceau, M., 188
Cœur-de-Lion, Richard, 185
Coleridge, 2, 212 ; " The
Ancient Mariner," 43 ; in-
troduction to the "A.M."
quoted, 217
Collins, William, 49
Combe, William, " Satires,"
62
Conrad, Joseph, 212
Courthope, W. J., 50, 56, 57
Cowley, Abraham, his prose,
210
Cowper, William, 49
Crystal Palace, The, 35, 63

D'ANNUNZIO, Gabriele,
191, 197-209
Darwin, Charles, 33
Davidson, John, quoted, 25 ;
his subjects, 35
Day, Jeffrey, " On the Wings
of the Morning," 29
De la Mare, Walter, " Fare-
well," 45
De Quincey, quoted, 218